100 FACTS ABOUT ASIA

Welcome to **100 Facts About Asia** a captivating journey through the heart of the world's largest and most diverse continent.

In these pages, you will embark on an enlightening exploration of Asia's incredible history, culture, and natural wonders. From the timeless majesty of the Taj Mahal to the architectural marvels of the Great Wall of China, from the vibrant street life of Tokyo to the tranquility of Bhutan, each fact will reveal a unique facet of this remarkable continent.

Whether you're an avid traveler, a history enthusiast, a food lover, or simply curious about the world, this book promises to be an engaging and educational voyage through the fascinating tapestry of Asia. *So, turn the page, and let's begin our journey, one fact at a time.*

The Maldives is a tropical paradise known for its stunning coral atolls and underwater resorts, offering a once-in-a-lifetime experience for travelers.

The city of Kyoto, Japan, is home to thousands of Shinto shrines and Buddhist temples, each with its unique history and cultural significance.

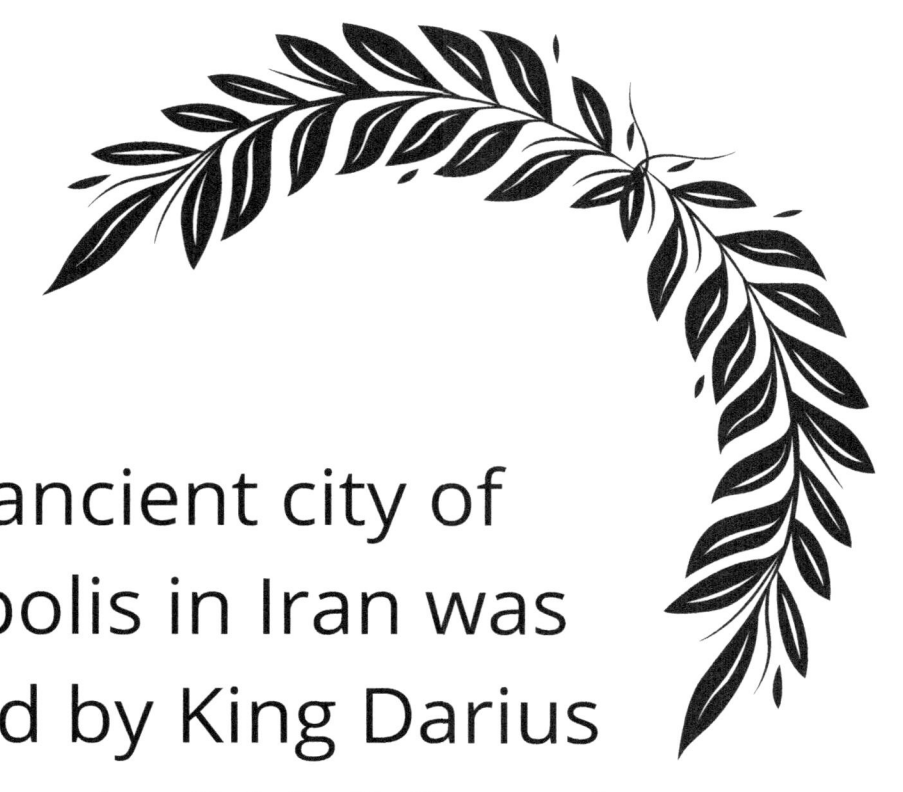

The ancient city of Persepolis in Iran was founded by King Darius the Great in 518 BC and served as a grand ceremonial center of the Persian Empire.

The Arabian Desert spans multiple countries, including Saudi Arabia, Oman, Yemen, and the United Arab Emirates, covering a vast expanse of the Arabian Peninsula.

Dubai's Palm Islands are artificial islands shaped like palm trees and the world map, constructed through ambitious engineering projects.

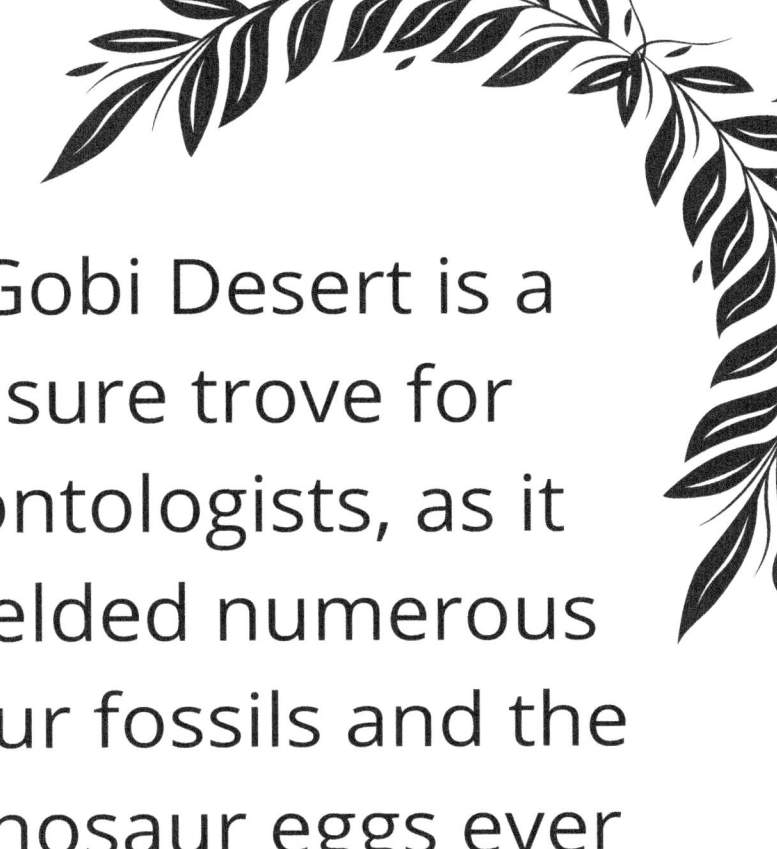

The Gobi Desert is a treasure trove for paleontologists, as it has yielded numerous dinosaur fossils and the first dinosaur eggs ever discovered.

The city of Lhasa in Tibet is famous for its historic monasteries, including the iconic Potala Palace, once the winter residence of the Dalai Lama.

The Arabian Desert is not just a barren wasteland; it supports unique desert flora and fauna, including the Arabian leopard and Arabian oryx.

The ancient city of Petra, Jordan, was carved into the rose-red cliffs of southern Jordan, creating a breathtaking blend of natural and man-made beauty.

The city of Mumbai, India, is home to the Bollywood film industry, producing the highest number of movies globally and attracting film enthusiasts worldwide.

The Gobi Desert covers an area roughly the size of France and is known for its dramatic landscapes, with towering sand dunes and rocky outcrops.

South Korea is a global leader in technology and innovation, with companies like Samsung, LG, and Hyundai making a significant impact on various industries.

The city of Dubai is known for its luxury shopping malls, such as Mall of the Emirates, which houses Ski Dubai, the Middle East's first indoor ski resort.

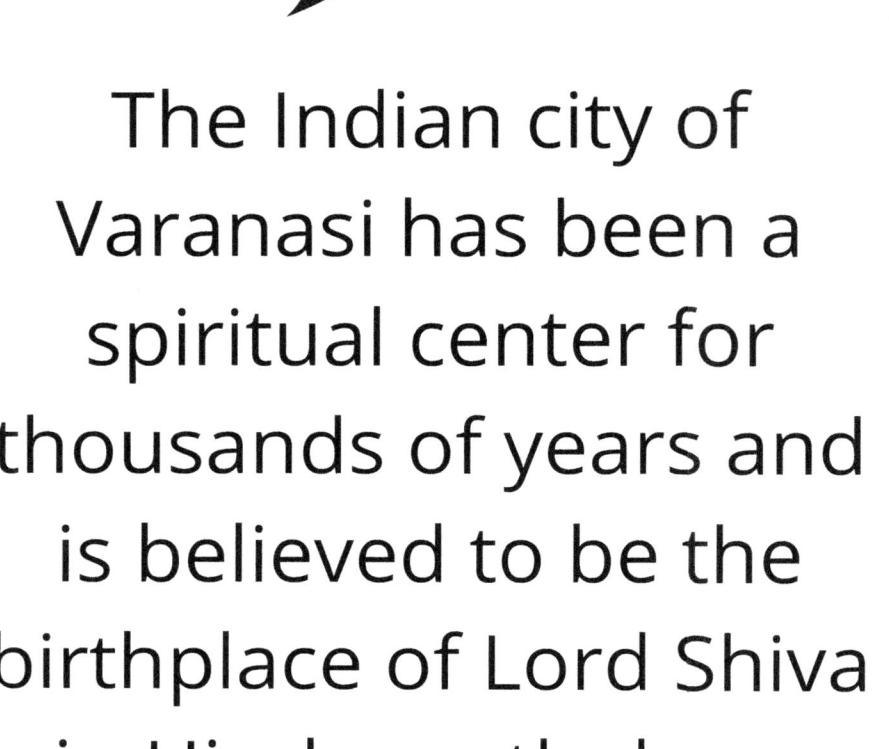

The Indian city of Varanasi has been a spiritual center for thousands of years and is believed to be the birthplace of Lord Shiva in Hindu mythology.

Sri Lanka, an island nation, boasts diverse ecosystems, from lush rainforests to arid plains, and is home to an array of unique wildlife, including the elusive Sri Lankan leopard.

The Karakoram Highway, one of the world's highest paved roads, offers breathtaking views of the Karakoram Range, including towering peaks like K2.

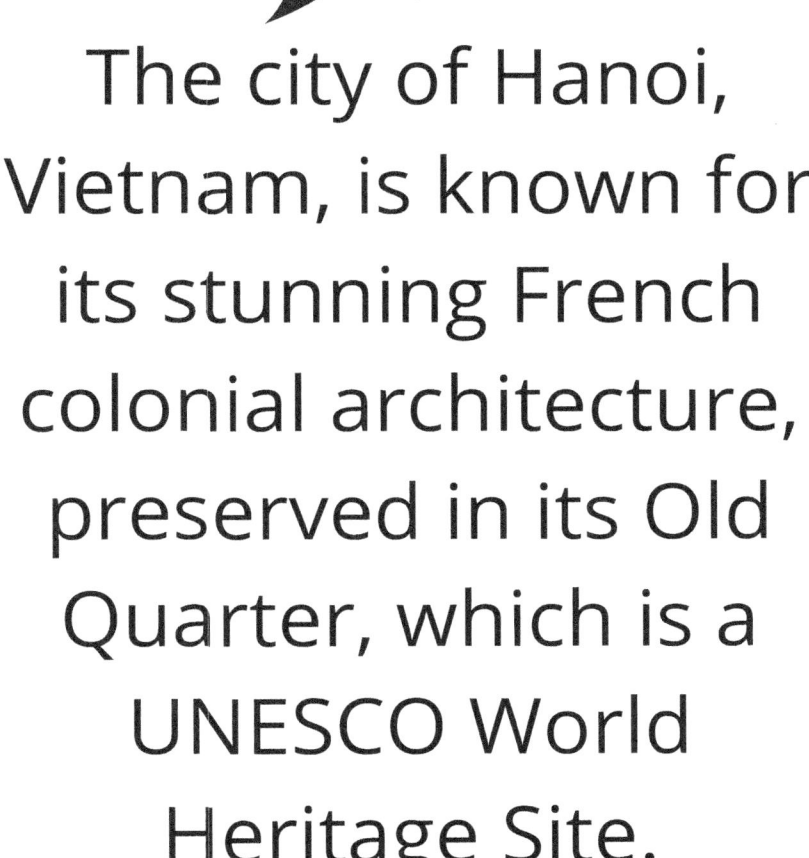

The city of Hanoi, Vietnam, is known for its stunning French colonial architecture, preserved in its Old Quarter, which is a UNESCO World Heritage Site.

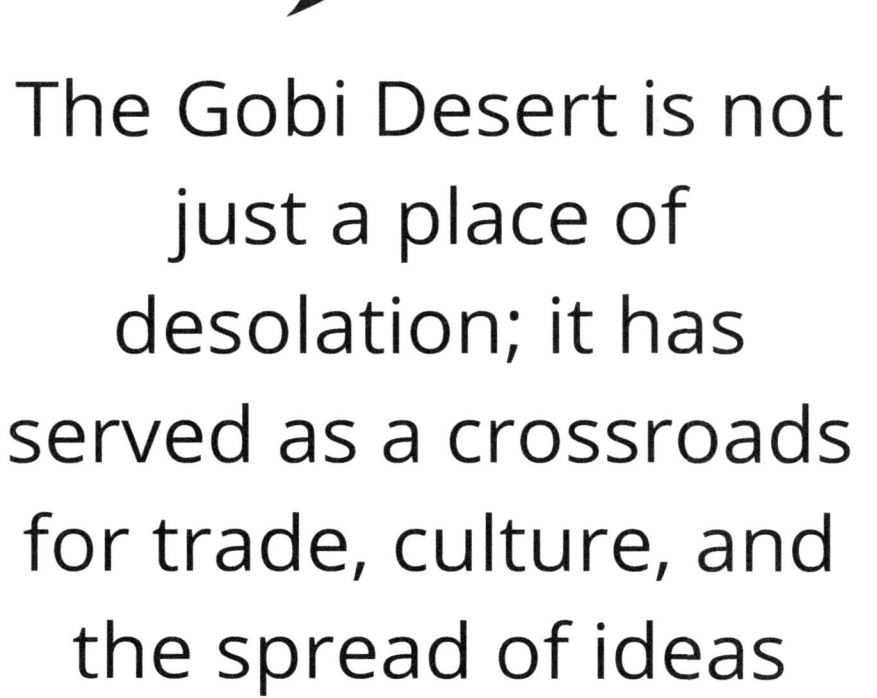

The Gobi Desert is not just a place of desolation; it has served as a crossroads for trade, culture, and the spread of ideas throughout history.

The ancient city of Kyoto, Japan, is a living museum of Japanese history and culture, with well-preserved traditional architecture and serene gardens.

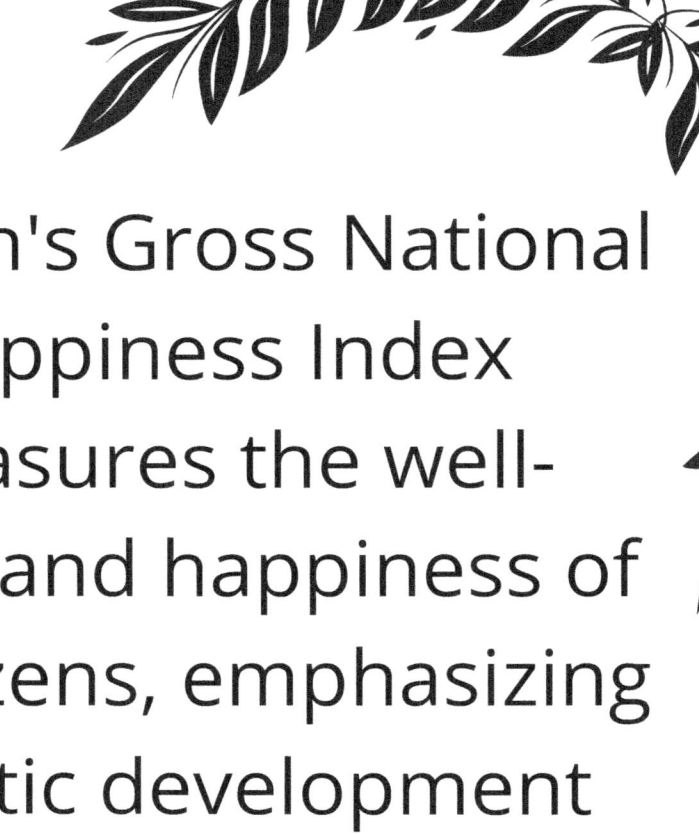

Bhutan's Gross National Happiness Index measures the well-being and happiness of its citizens, emphasizing holistic development over economic growth.

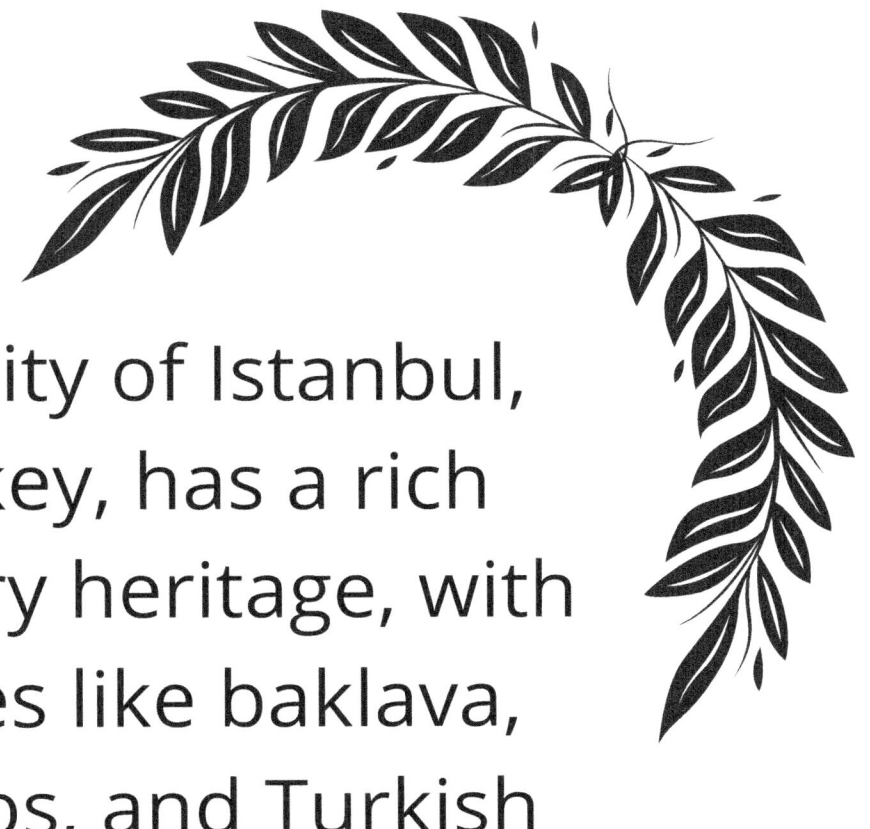

The city of Istanbul, Turkey, has a rich culinary heritage, with dishes like baklava, kebabs, and Turkish delight, delighting taste buds for centuries.

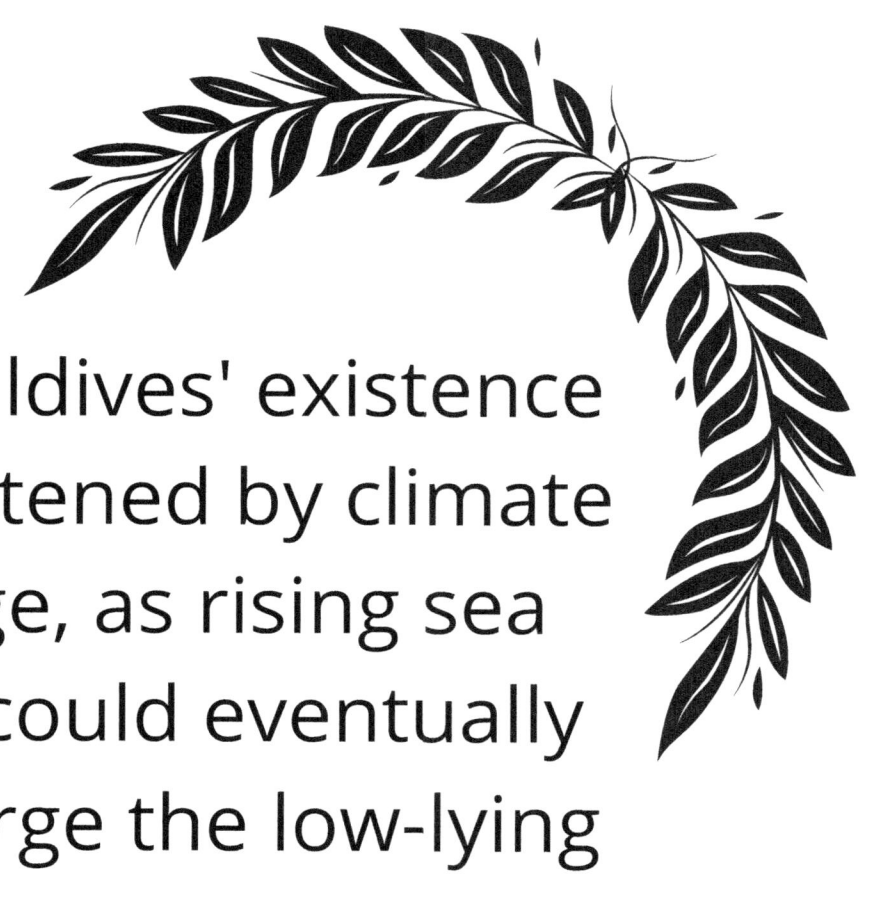

The Maldives' existence is threatened by climate change, as rising sea levels could eventually submerge the low-lying atolls.

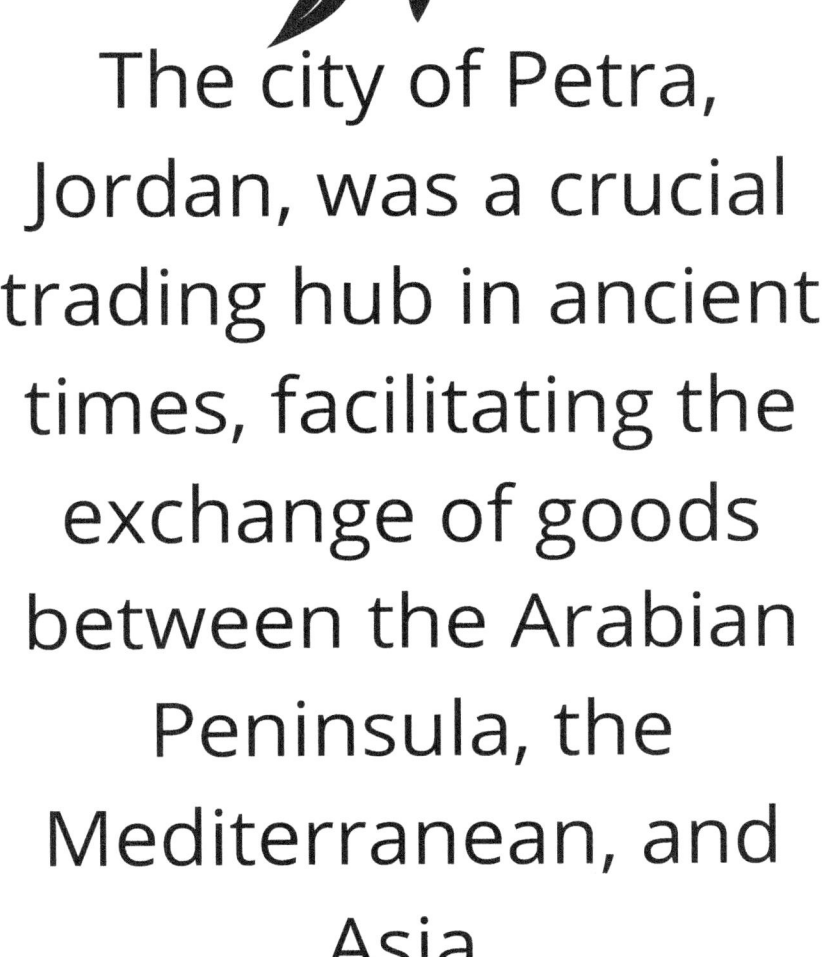

The city of Petra, Jordan, was a crucial trading hub in ancient times, facilitating the exchange of goods between the Arabian Peninsula, the Mediterranean, and Asia.

The Great Wall of China's construction spanned centuries, with various dynasties adding sections to protect against invasions from northern nomadic tribes.

The Maldives is known for its luxurious overwater bungalows, where guests can wake up to the sights and sounds of the Indian Ocean.

The city of Dubai, United Arab Emirates, has become synonymous with architectural marvels, such as the Burj Khalifa, which stands at over 2,700 feet (828 meters).

The Arabian Desert's harsh climate has shaped the region's culture and traditions, with communities developed around the availability of water sources.

The city of Varanasi, India, is steeped in spirituality and is believed to be a place of salvation for those who die and are cremated on its sacred ghats.

The Maldives is a prime destination for water sports enthusiasts, offering opportunities for snorkeling, scuba diving, windsurfing, and more.

The city of Istanbul, Turkey, is renowned for its historic bazaars, such as the Grand Bazaar, where visitors can haggle for unique souvenirs and spices.

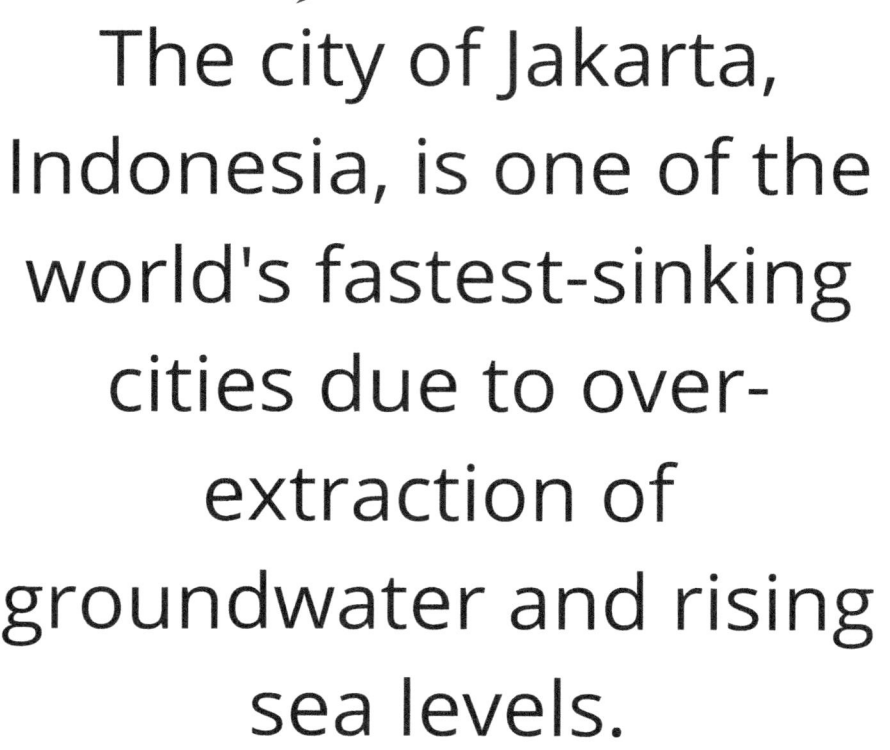

The city of Jakarta, Indonesia, is one of the world's fastest-sinking cities due to over-extraction of groundwater and rising sea levels.

The Arabian Desert is known for its vast "seas" of sand dunes, including the Rub' al Khali, the world's largest continuous sand desert.

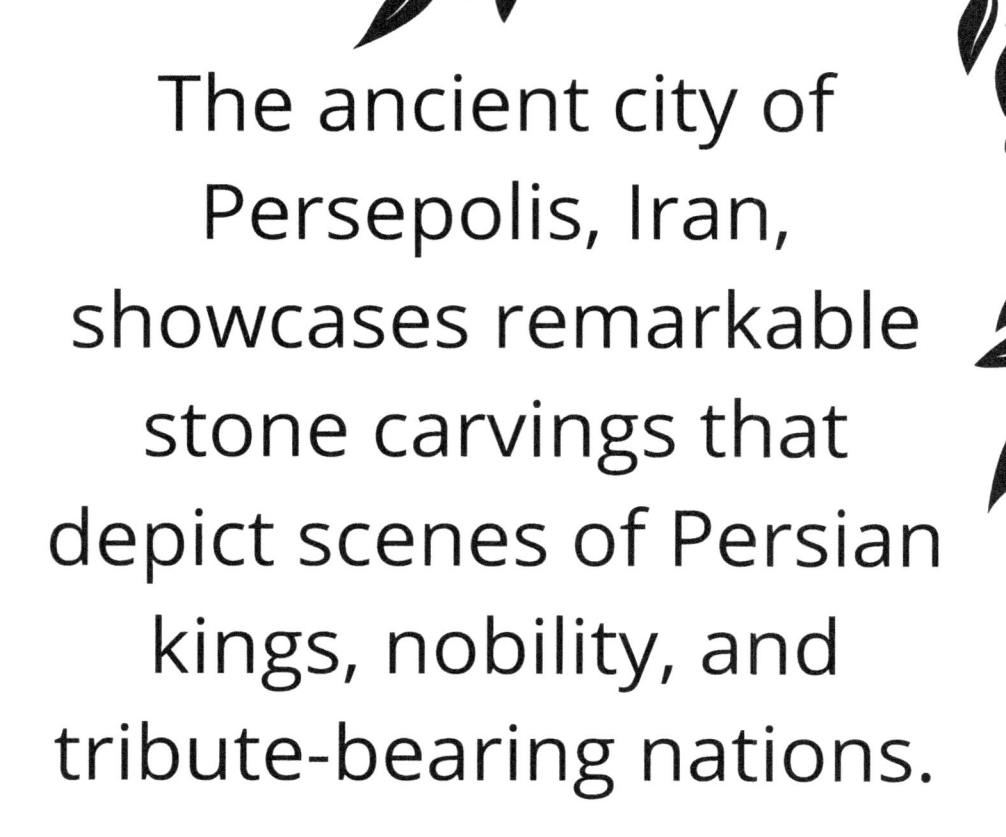

The ancient city of Persepolis, Iran, showcases remarkable stone carvings that depict scenes of Persian kings, nobility, and tribute-bearing nations.

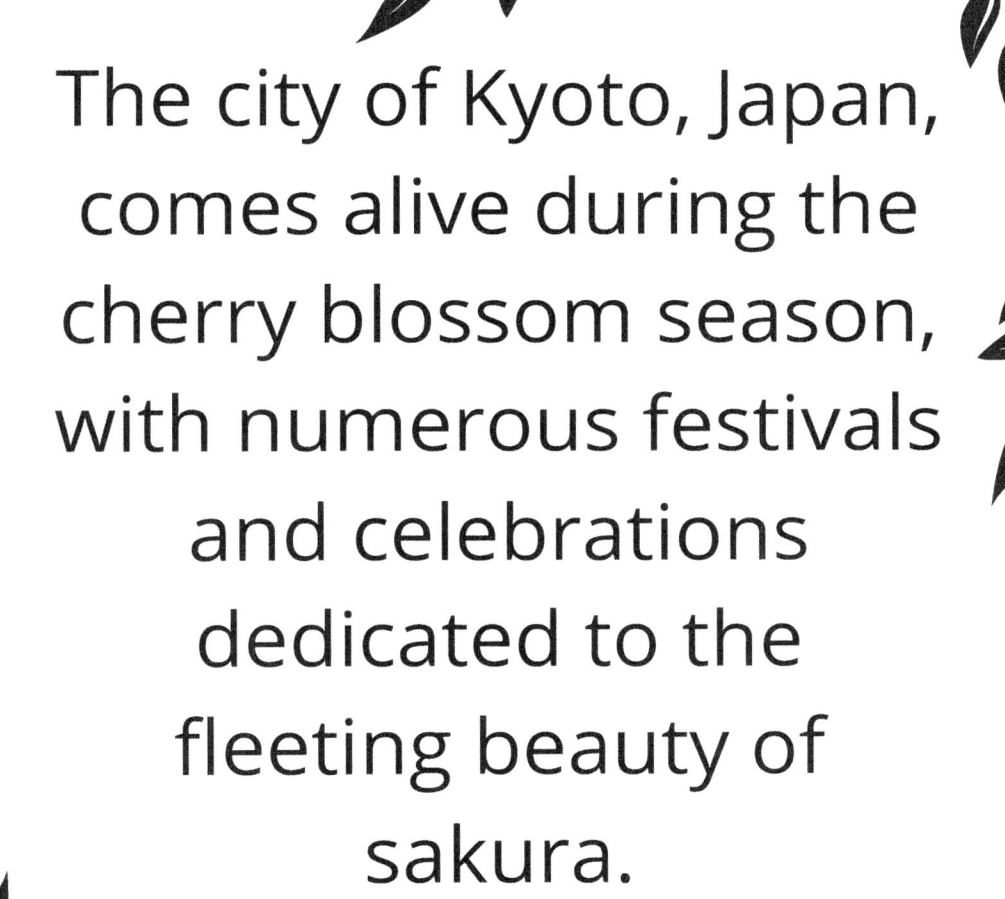

The city of Kyoto, Japan, comes alive during the cherry blossom season, with numerous festivals and celebrations dedicated to the fleeting beauty of sakura.

The Maldives is a renowned honeymoon destination, offering couples the chance to escape to private, secluded island resorts.

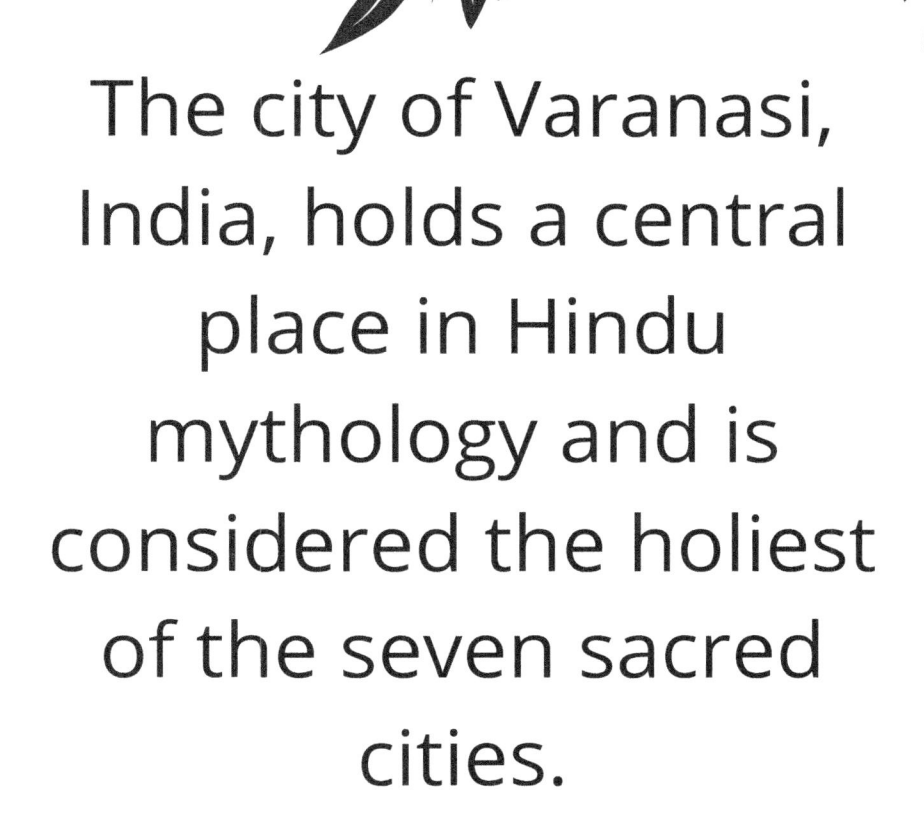

The city of Varanasi, India, holds a central place in Hindu mythology and is considered the holiest of the seven sacred cities.

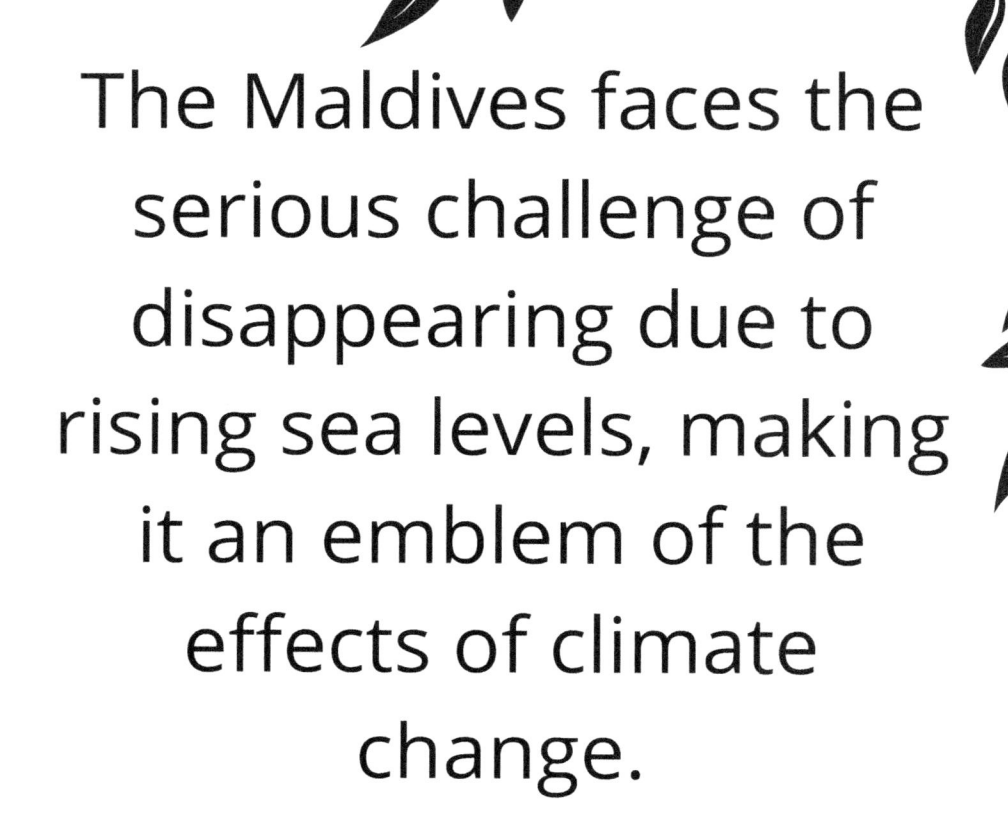

The Maldives faces the serious challenge of disappearing due to rising sea levels, making it an emblem of the effects of climate change.

The Arabian Desert is a vast expanse of arid land, with sand dunes reaching up to 800 feet (244 meters) in height.

The Great Mosque of Mecca, surrounded by the Masjid al-Haram, can accommodate over a million worshippers during the Hajj pilgrimage.

The city of Petra, Jordan, has long been a center for trade and commerce, connecting the Arabian Peninsula, Asia, and Europe.

The Arabian Desert is home to the stunning Wadi Rum, a protected desert wilderness famous for its unique rock formations and red sand dunes.

The ancient city of Persepolis, Iran, is a UNESCO World Heritage Site and a testament to the grandeur of the Persian Empire.

The Maldives is a nation comprised of 26 coral atolls, each consisting of numerous islands and islets.

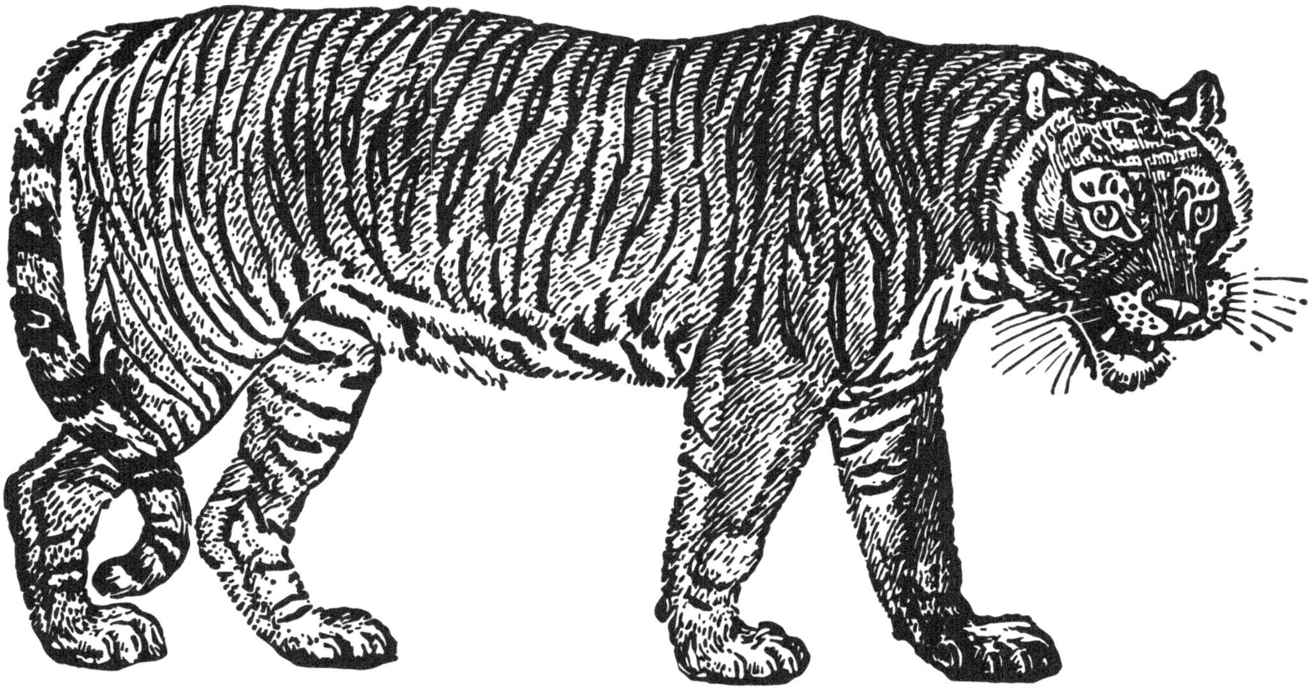

The city of Kyoto, Japan, showcases the blending of ancient traditions and modern life, with geisha culture coexisting with contemporary urban developments.

Bhutan's commitment to Gross National Happiness reflects its prioritization of holistic well-being over economic growth, focusing on sustainable development.

The city of Dubai, United Arab Emirates, is known for its luxurious hotels, including the Burj Al Arab, often called the world's only "7-star" hotel.

The Great Mosque of Mecca is the epicenter of Islam, drawing millions of pilgrims each year during the Hajj pilgrimage.

The Arabian Desert is home to the Empty Quarter, or Rub' al Khali, a vast area of undulating sand dunes, some of which reach over 800 feet (244 meters) in height.

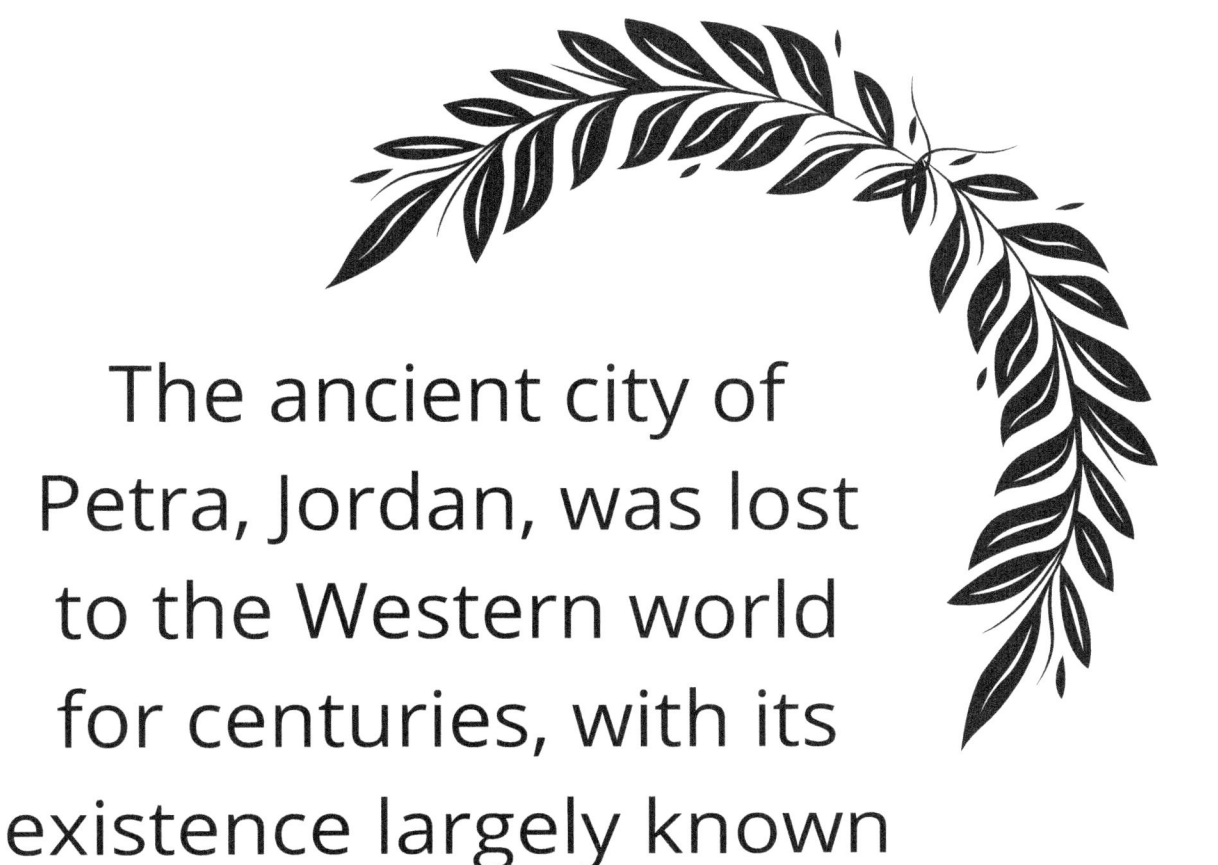

The ancient city of Petra, Jordan, was lost to the Western world for centuries, with its existence largely known only to the local Bedouin people.

The Arabian Desert's vast dunes, such as those in the Rub' al Khali, create an otherworldly landscape that has been featured in films like "Lawrence of Arabia."

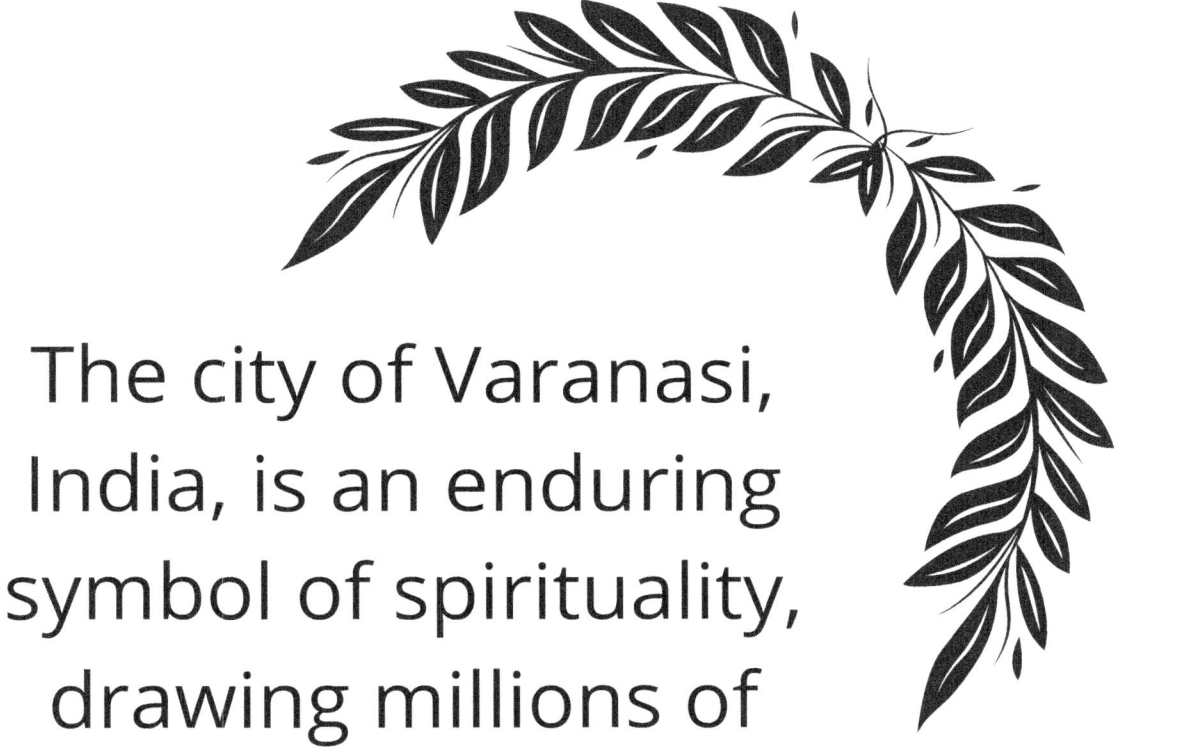

The city of Varanasi, India, is an enduring symbol of spirituality, drawing millions of pilgrims and travelers seeking a spiritual experience.

The Maldives' crystal-clear waters are home to an abundance of marine life, including colorful coral reefs, tropical fish, and even gentle whale sharks.

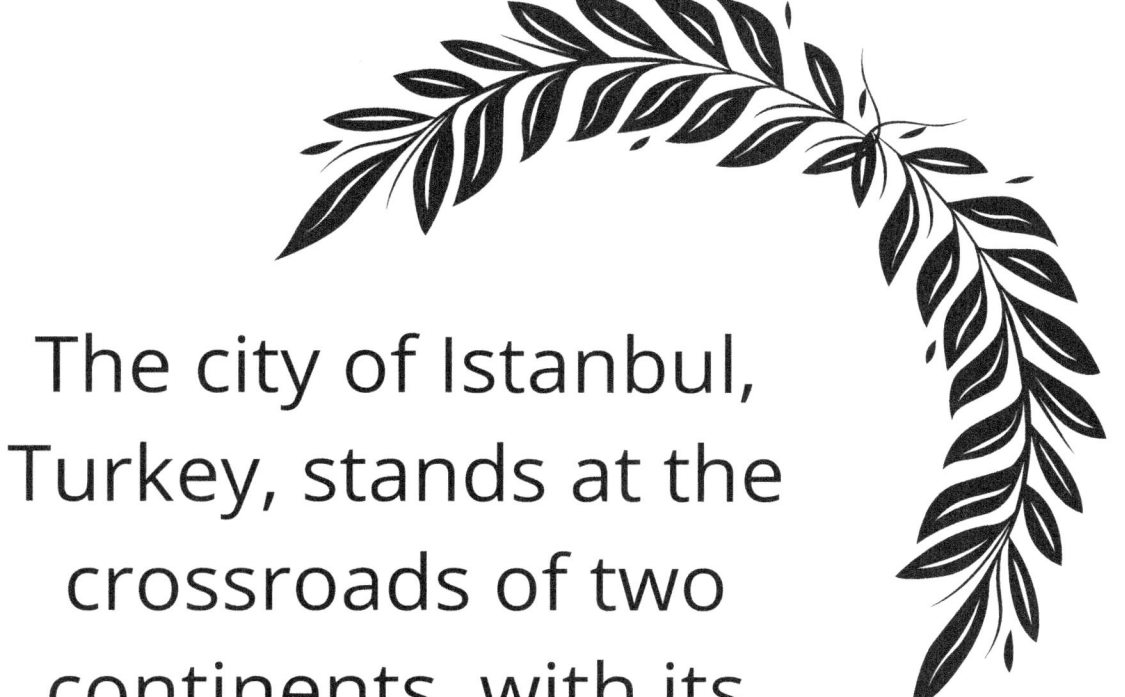

The city of Istanbul, Turkey, stands at the crossroads of two continents, with its European and Asian sides connected by the Bosphorus Bridge.

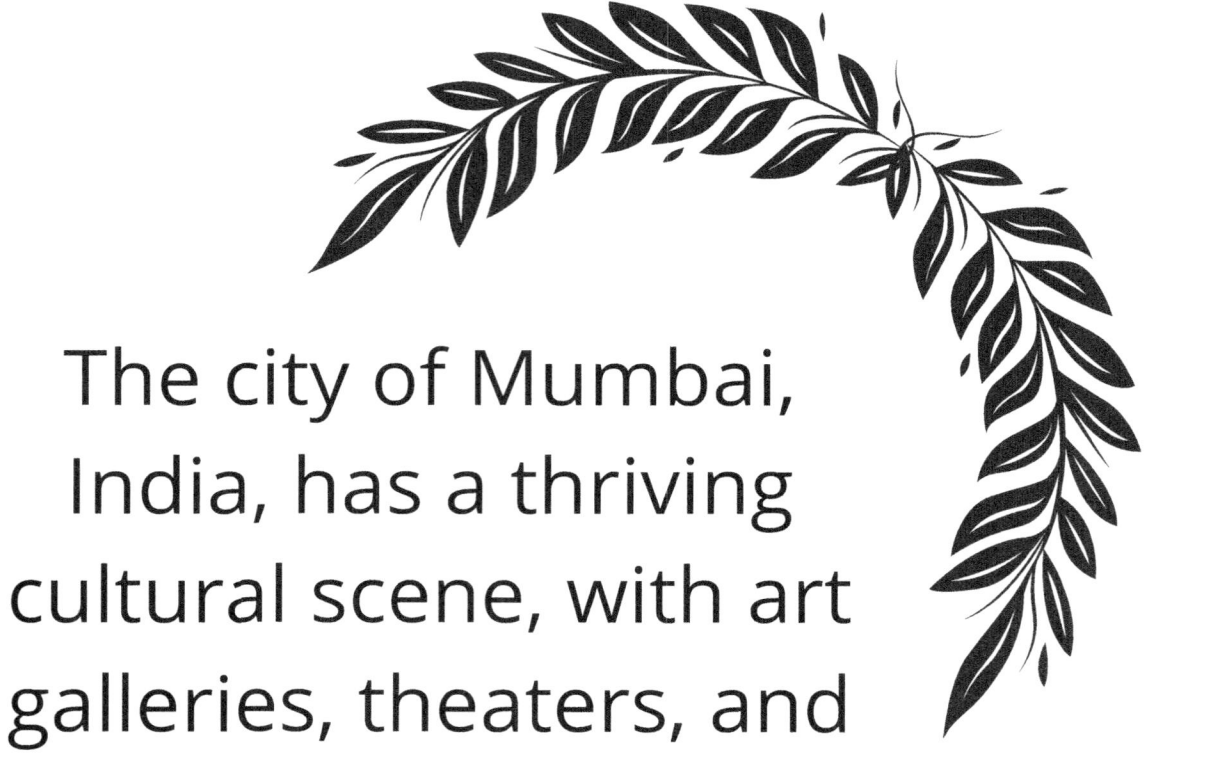

The city of Mumbai, India, has a thriving cultural scene, with art galleries, theaters, and a lively music industry, in addition to its film production.

The Karakoram Highway is an engineering marvel, traversing some of the most rugged terrain on Earth and providing access to remote mountain communities.

The city of Hanoi, Vietnam, is known for its vibrant street food culture, where you can savor dishes like pho and banh mi in local markets.

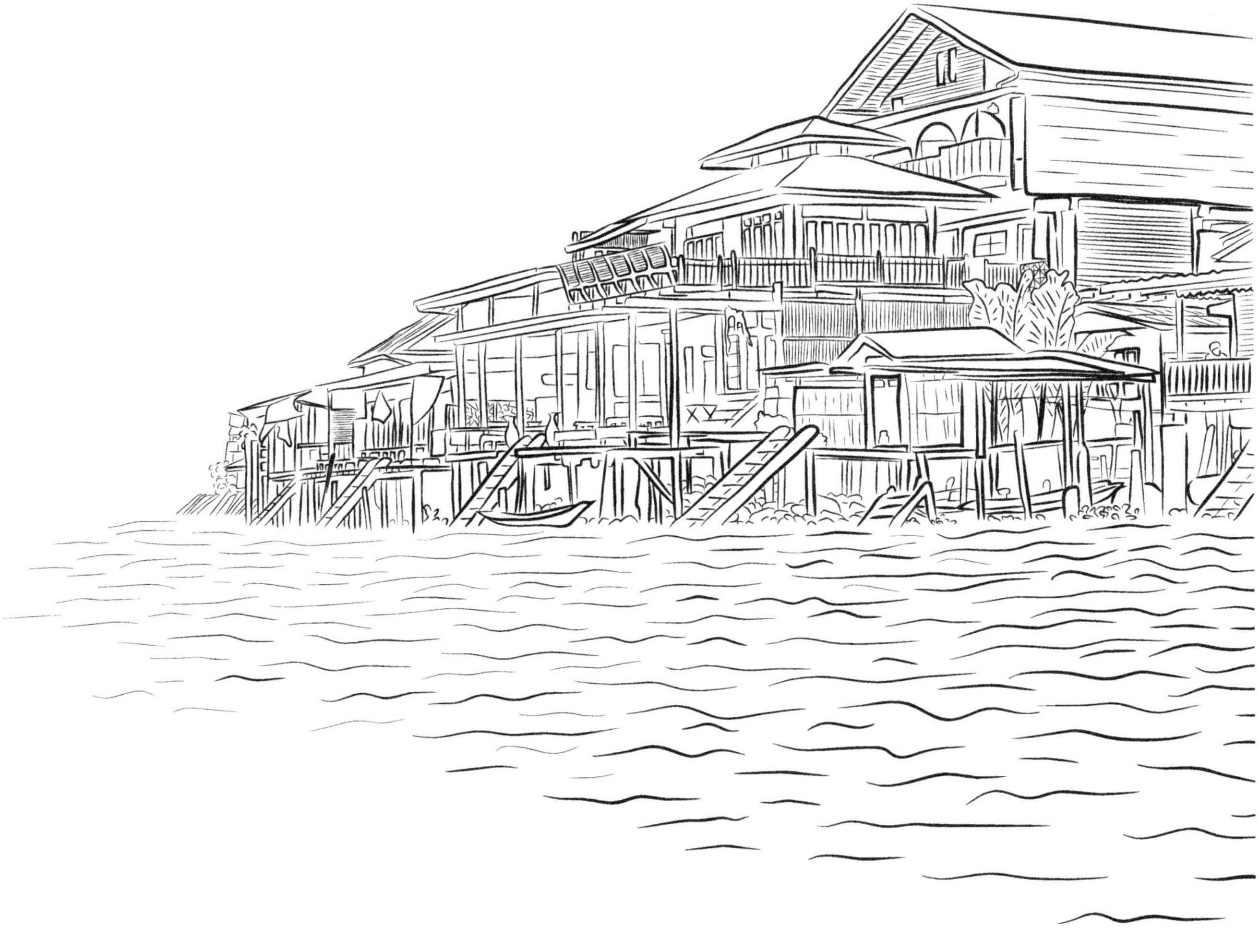

South Korea's DMZ, or Demilitarized Zone, has become a symbol of the division of the Korean Peninsula and the ongoing tension between North and South Korea.

The Gobi Desert is characterized by its extreme temperature variations, with scorching summers and frigid winters.

The ancient city of Kyoto, Japan, has a long history of traditional arts, including tea ceremonies, Ikebana (flower arranging), and Noh theater.

The Arabian Desert's harsh climate has fostered a unique way of life, with Bedouin communities historically relying on camel herding and trade.

The Maldives is a top destination for honeymooners, offering privacy and romance in luxurious overwater bungalows.

The city of Petra, Jordan, was once a vital trading center, connecting the Mediterranean with the Arabian Peninsula, Africa, and Asia.

The Great Wall of China is not a single continuous wall, but rather a system of walls, forts, and watchtowers built over different dynasties.

The Maldives faces the serious threat of disappearing due to rising sea levels, putting its unique ecosystems and cultures at risk.

The Arabian Desert is not just a vast expanse of sand; it features dramatic landscapes with deep canyons, rock formations, and oases.

The ancient city of Persepolis, Iran, features impressive stone carvings, reliefs, and inscriptions that provide insights into the history and culture of the Achaemenid Empire.

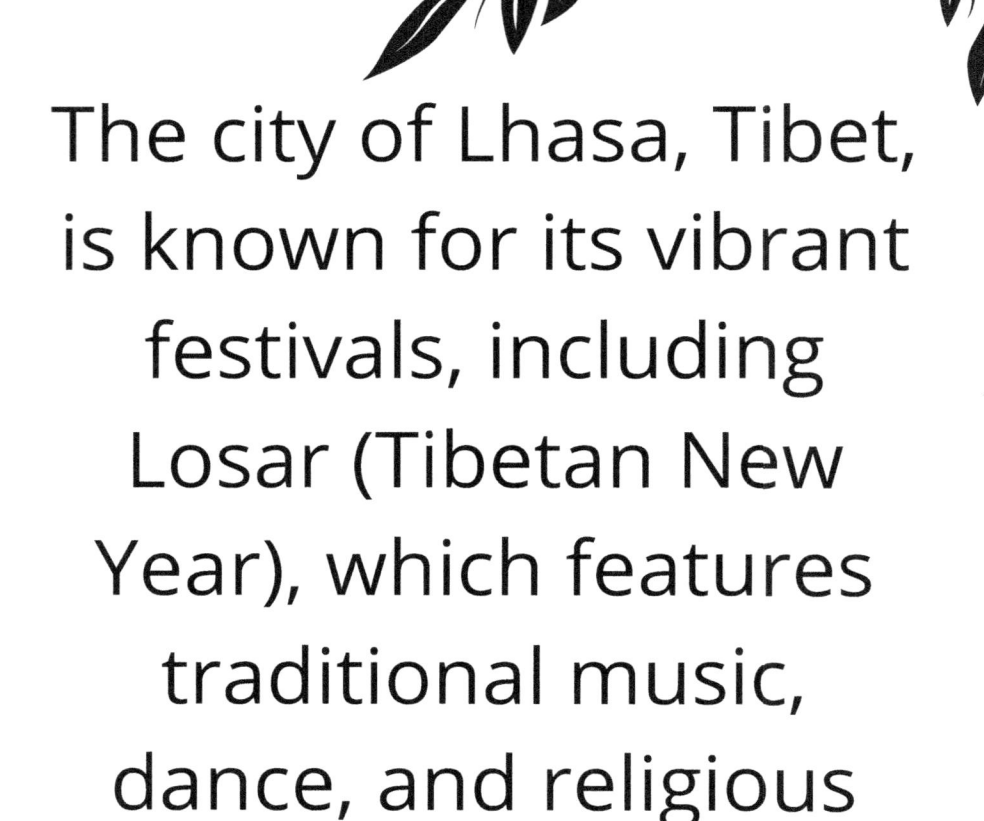

The city of Lhasa, Tibet, is known for its vibrant festivals, including Losar (Tibetan New Year), which features traditional music, dance, and religious rituals.

The Gobi Desert has played a significant role in the exchange of goods and culture along the Silk Road, connecting China with the West.

South Korea's technological innovations have made a global impact, with its smartphone and electronics industries influencing daily life worldwide.

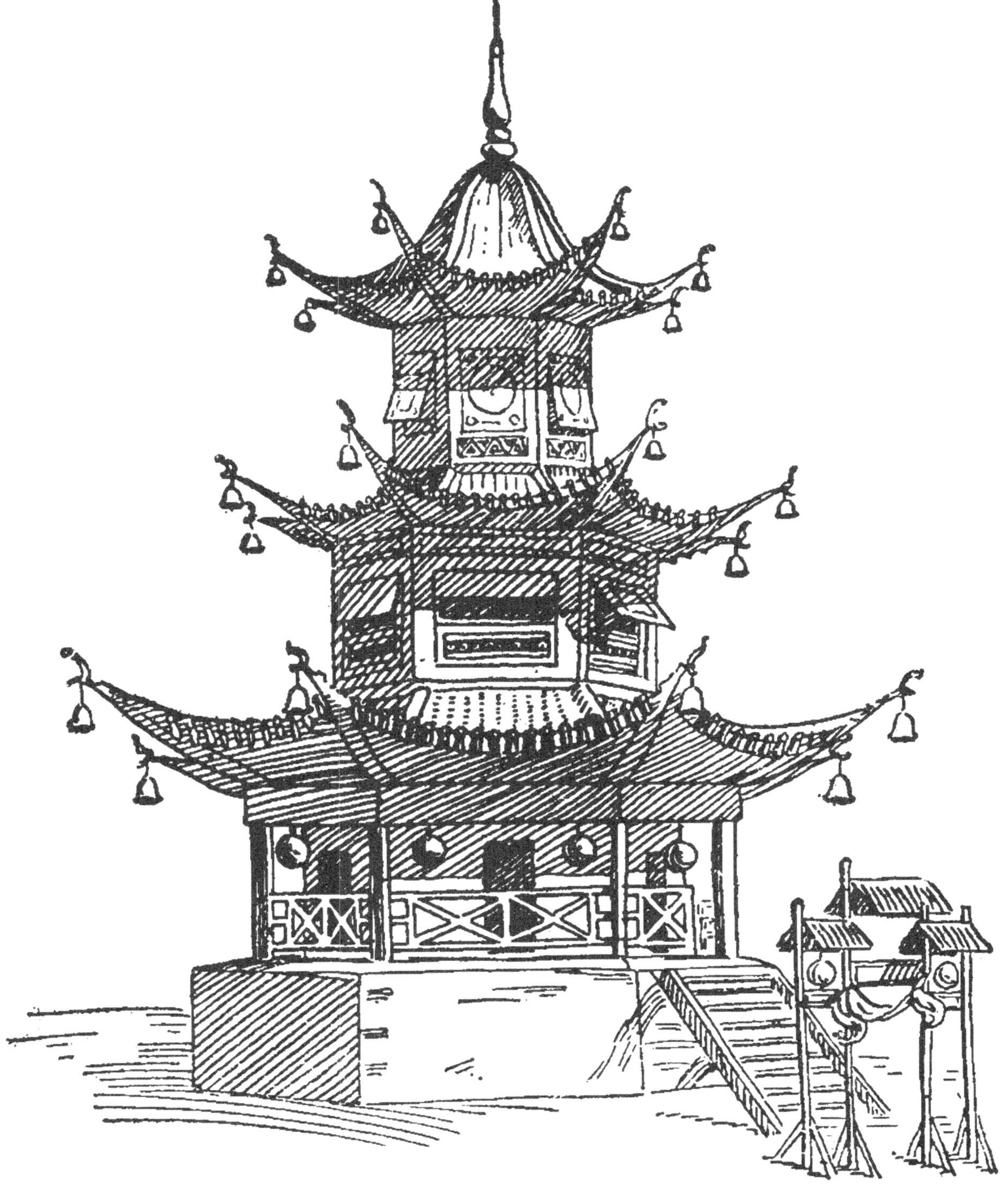

The city of Dubai, United Arab Emirates, is known for its architectural achievements, including the Palm Jumeirah, an artificial island shaped like a palm tree.

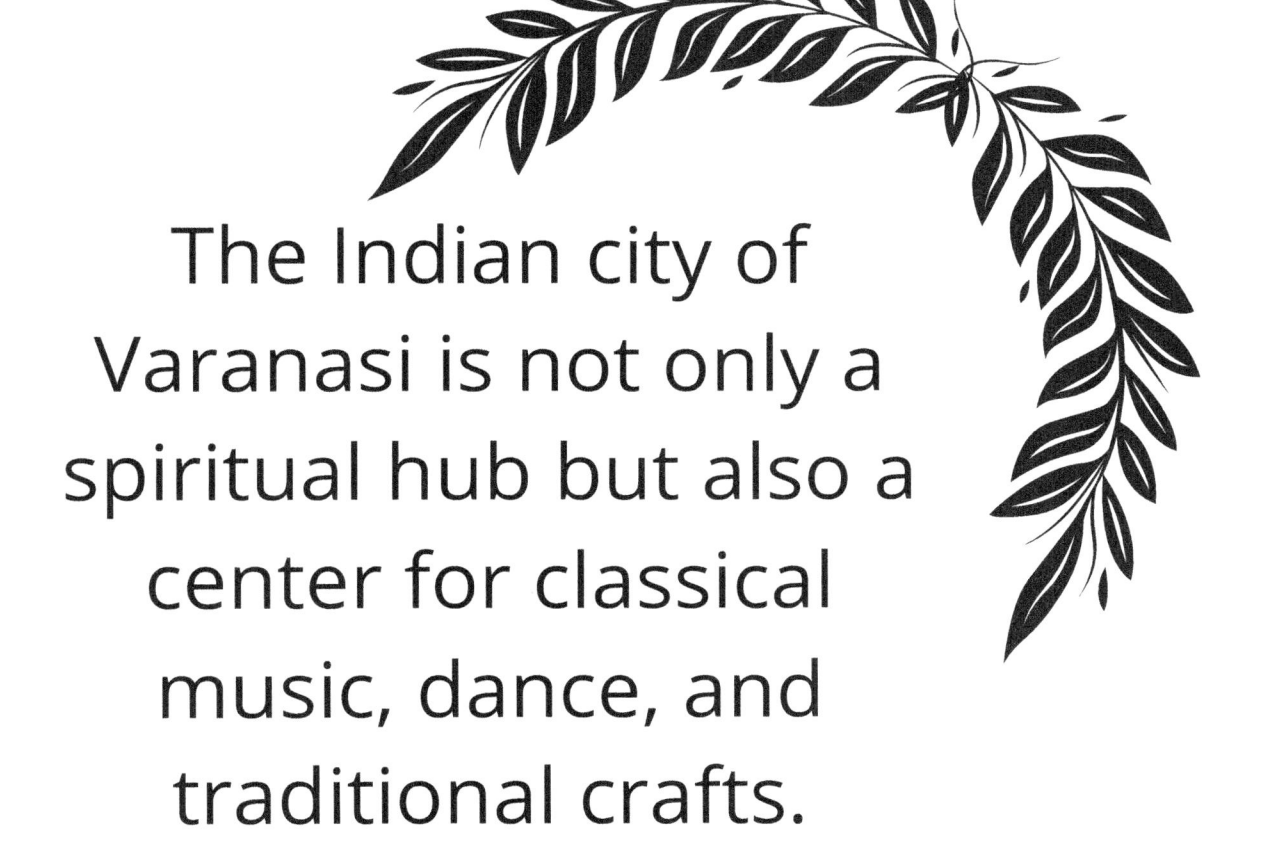

The Indian city of Varanasi is not only a spiritual hub but also a center for classical music, dance, and traditional crafts.

The Maldives' economy heavily depends on tourism, with this sector contributing significantly to the country's GDP.

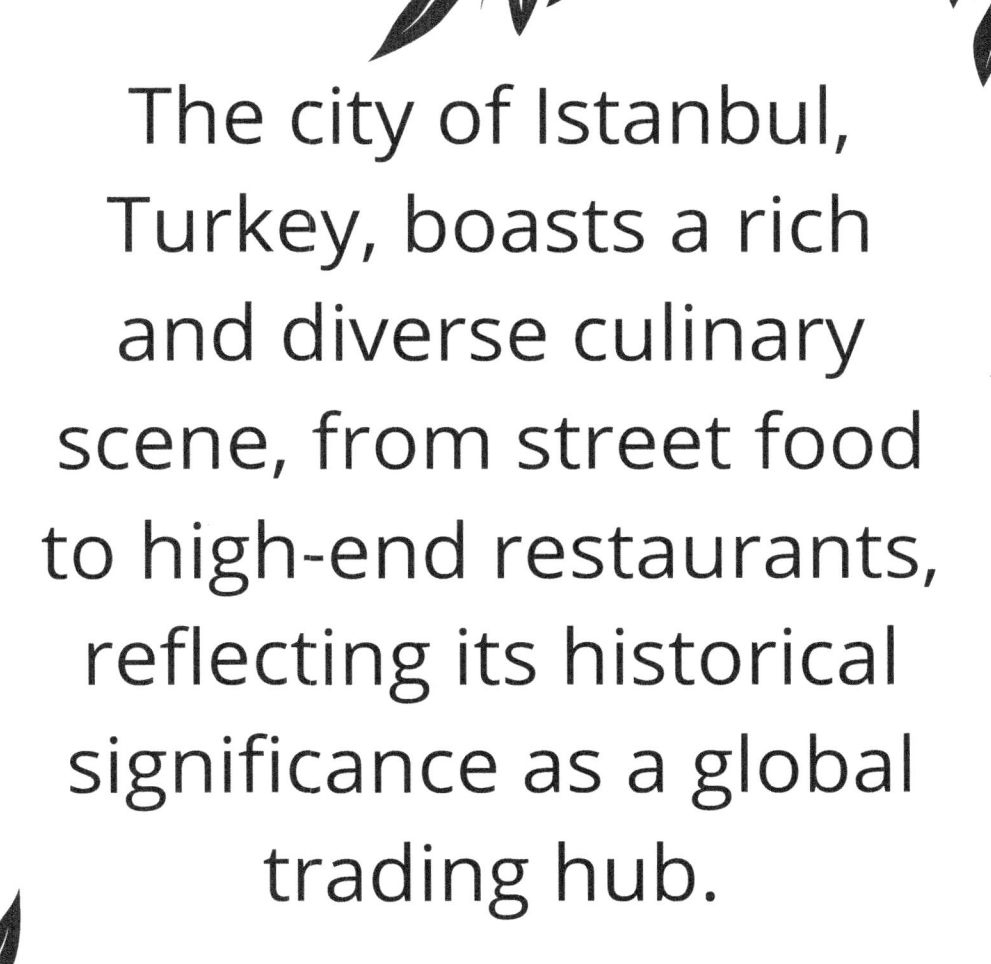

The city of Istanbul, Turkey, boasts a rich and diverse culinary scene, from street food to high-end restaurants, reflecting its historical significance as a global trading hub.

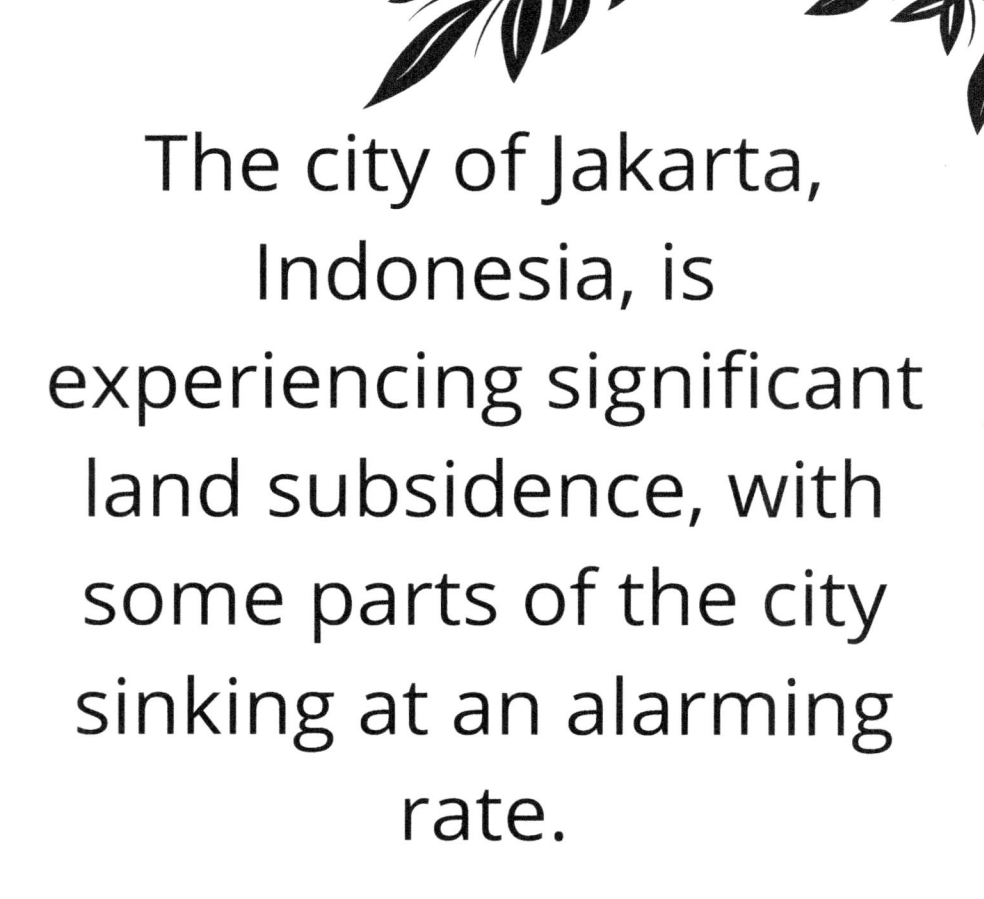

The city of Jakarta, Indonesia, is experiencing significant land subsidence, with some parts of the city sinking at an alarming rate.

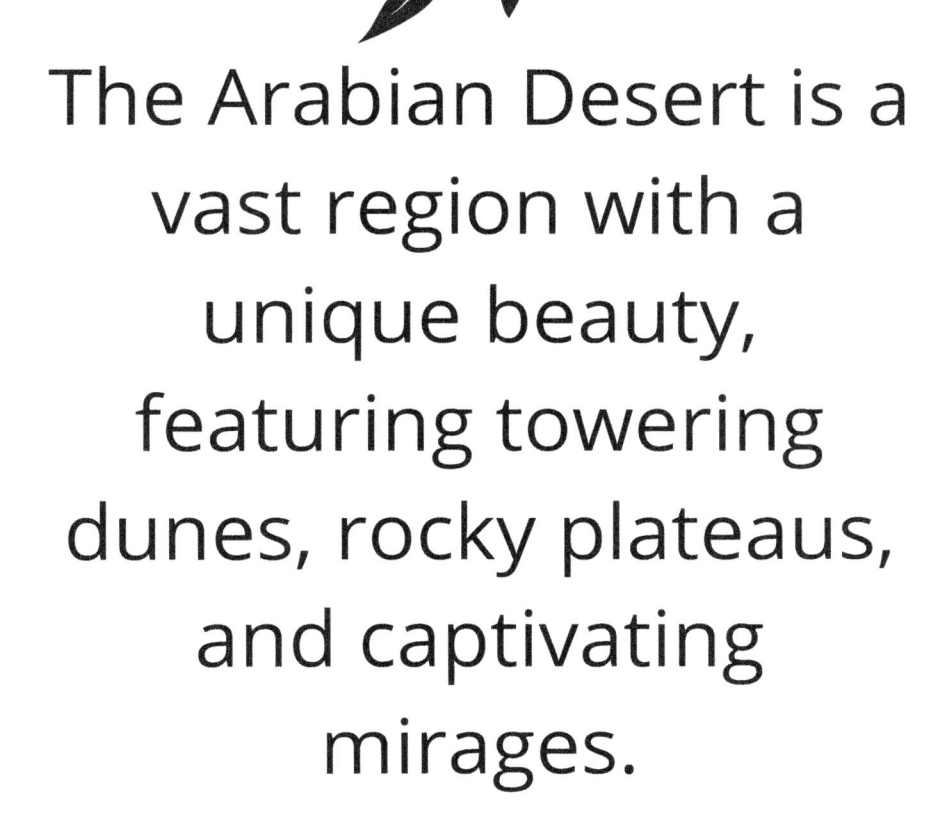

The Arabian Desert is a vast region with a unique beauty, featuring towering dunes, rocky plateaus, and captivating mirages.

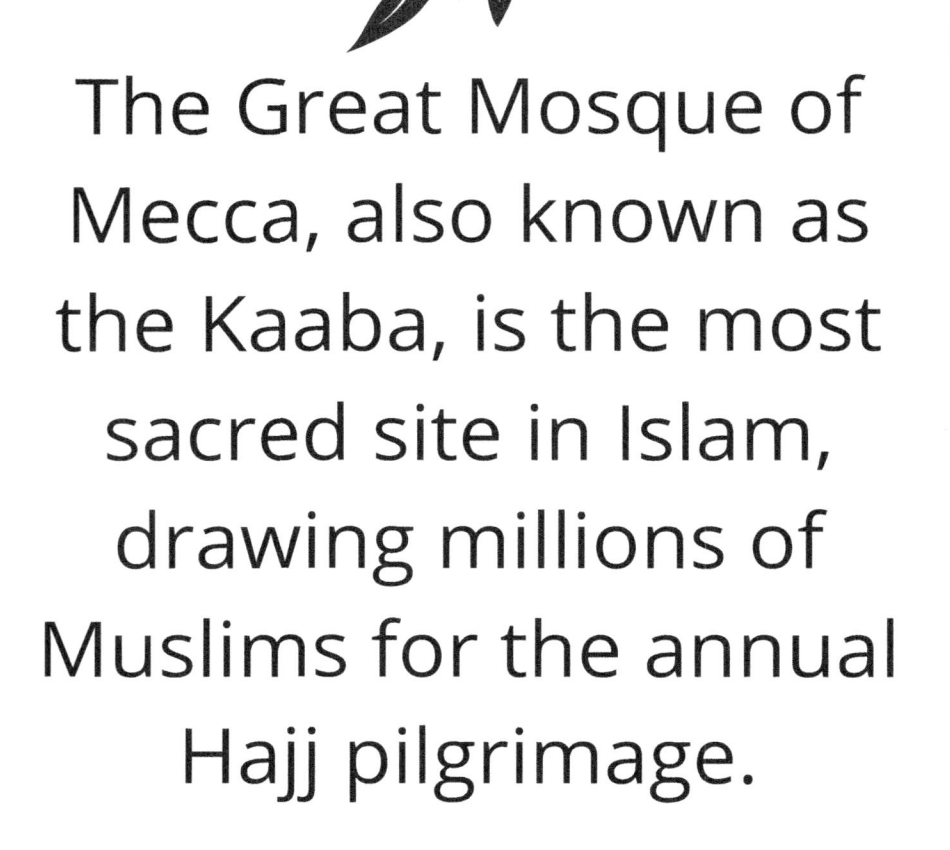

The Great Mosque of Mecca, also known as the Kaaba, is the most sacred site in Islam, drawing millions of Muslims for the annual Hajj pilgrimage.

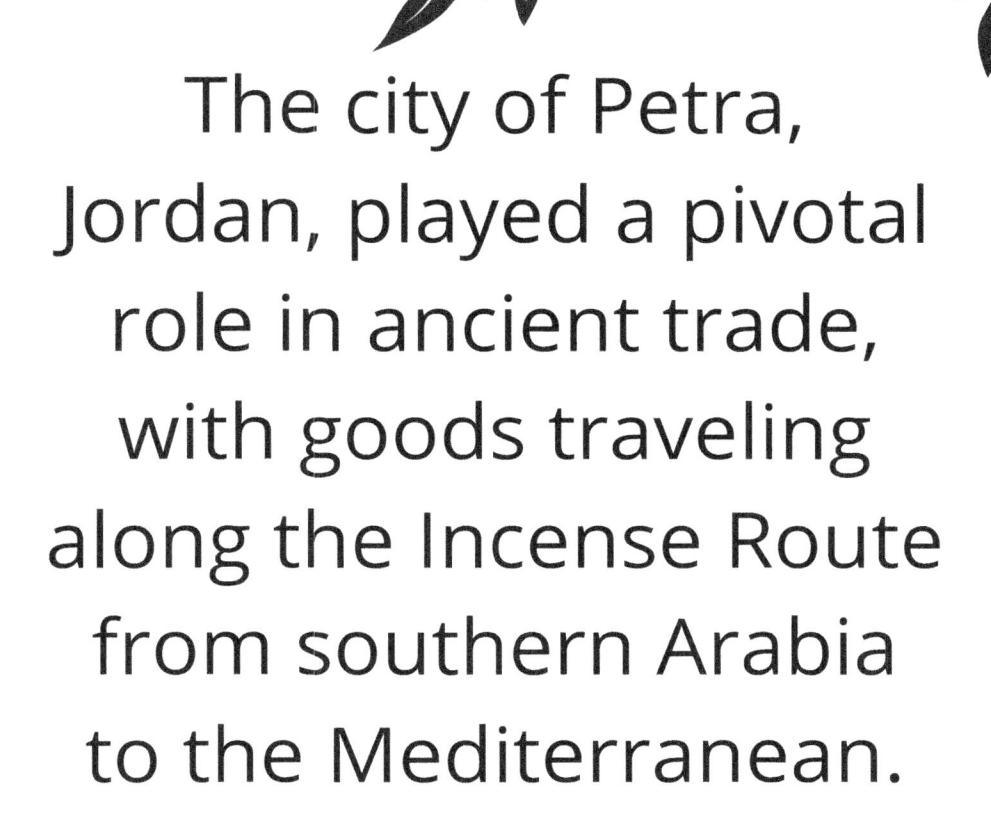

The city of Petra, Jordan, played a pivotal role in ancient trade, with goods traveling along the Incense Route from southern Arabia to the Mediterranean.

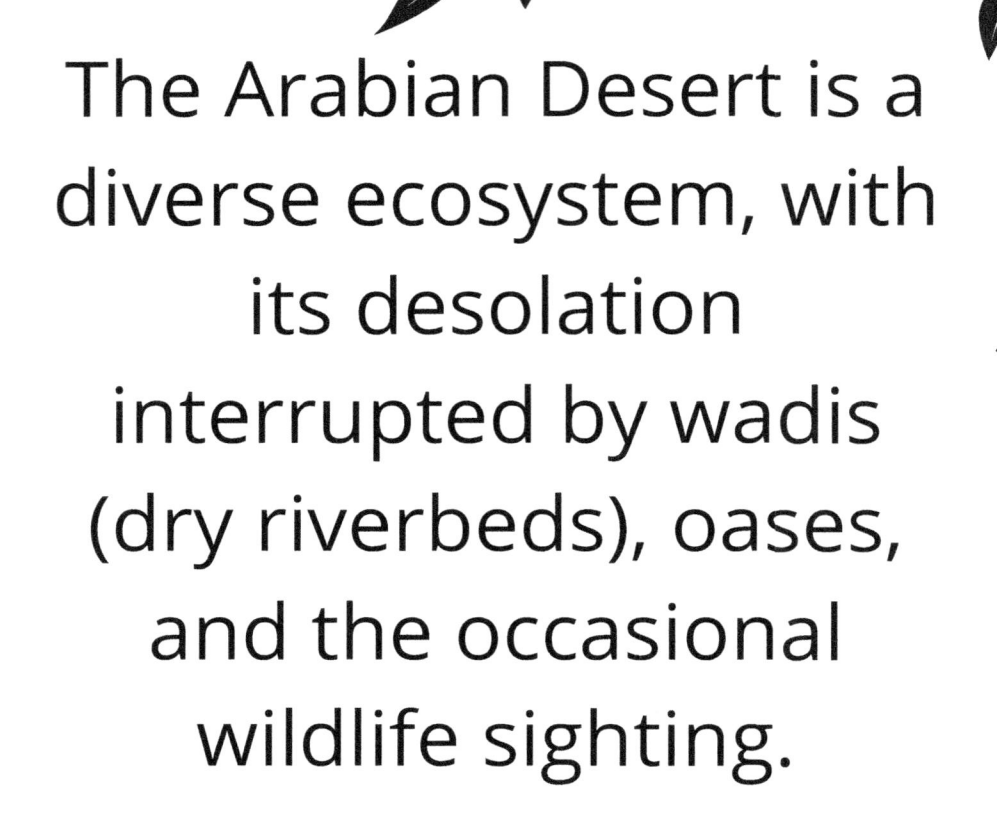

The Arabian Desert is a diverse ecosystem, with its desolation interrupted by wadis (dry riverbeds), oases, and the occasional wildlife sighting.

The ancient city of Persepolis, Iran, was destroyed by Alexander the Great in 330 BC, leading to the decline of the Achaemenid Empire.

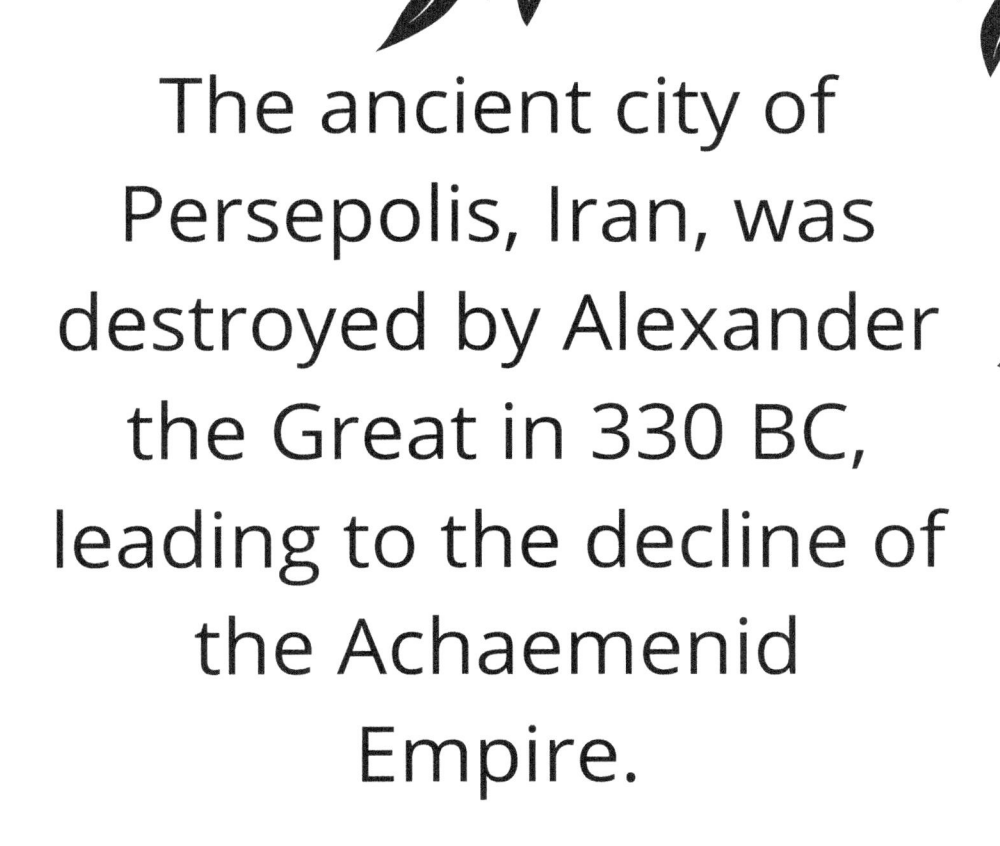

The Maldives is a nation threatened by climate change, with the rising sea levels endangering its very existence.

The city of Kyoto, Japan, offers a profound connection to the country's traditional arts, including the refined art of the tea ceremony.

Bhutan's Gross National Happiness Index measures aspects of well-being such as psychological well-being, health, education, and good governance.

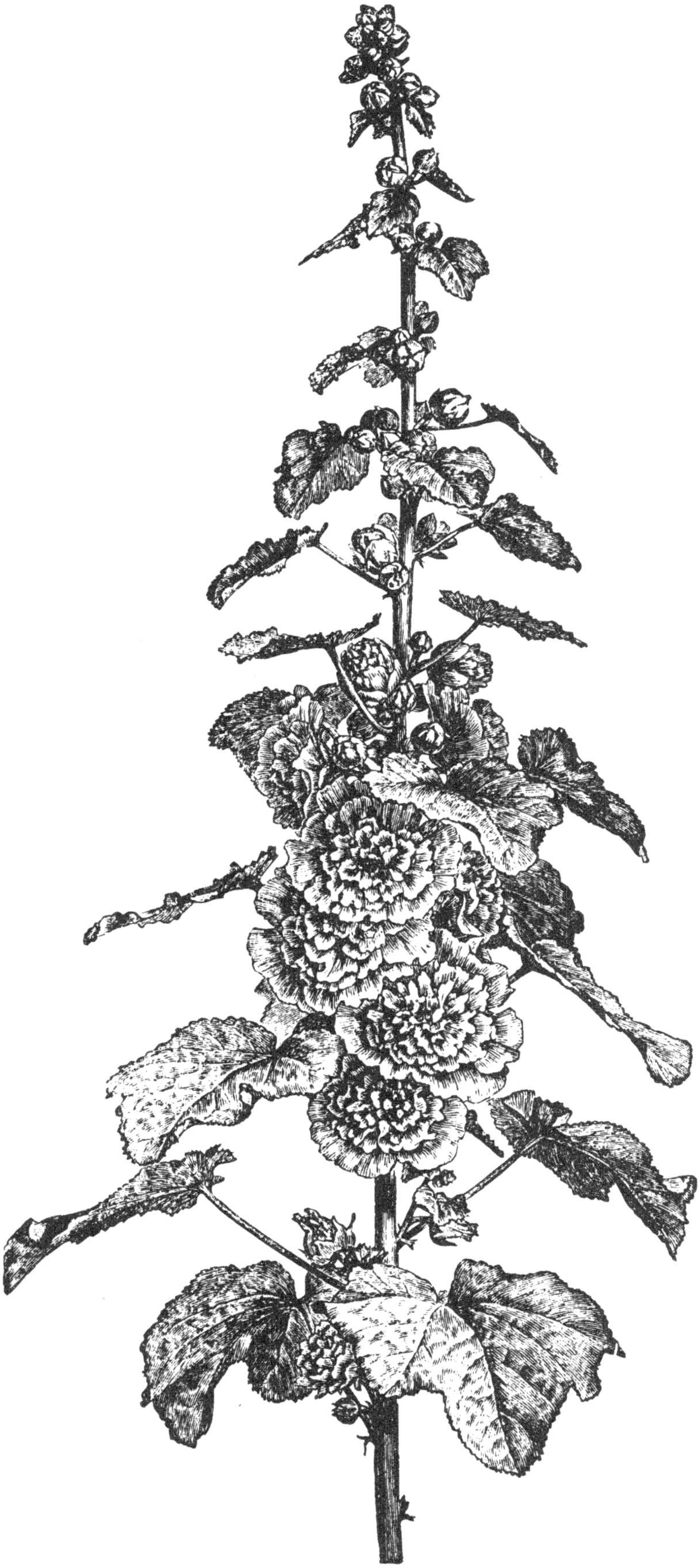

The Karakoram Highway, connecting Pakistan and China, offers breathtaking views of the Karakoram Range, home to some of the world's highest peaks.

The city of Hanoi, Vietnam, is famous for its delicious street food, where you can find dishes like bun cha and egg coffee.

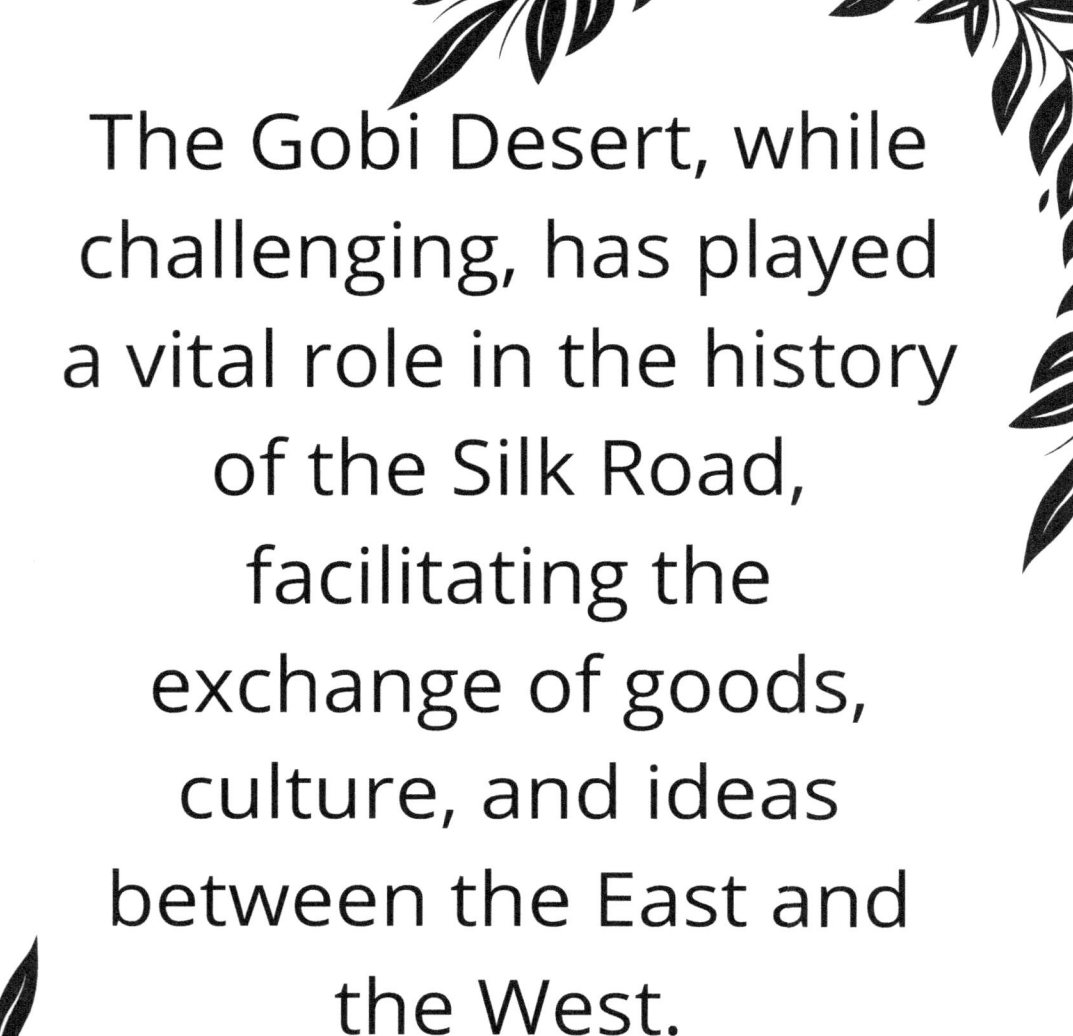

The Gobi Desert, while challenging, has played a vital role in the history of the Silk Road, facilitating the exchange of goods, culture, and ideas between the East and the West.

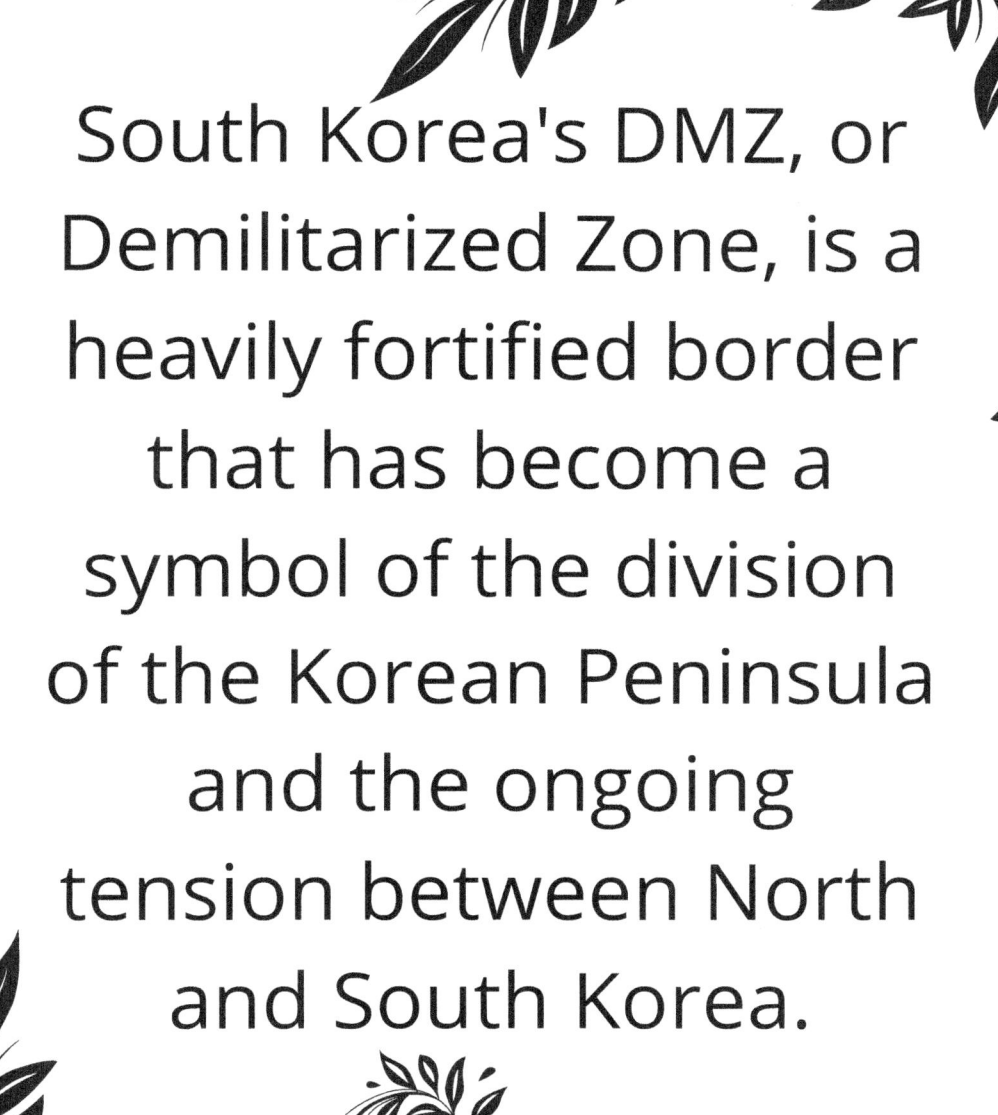

South Korea's DMZ, or Demilitarized Zone, is a heavily fortified border that has become a symbol of the division of the Korean Peninsula and the ongoing tension between North and South Korea.

The Great Wall of China has been expanded, rebuilt, and reinforced over many dynasties, making it a testament to the enduring history and engineering prowess of ancient China.

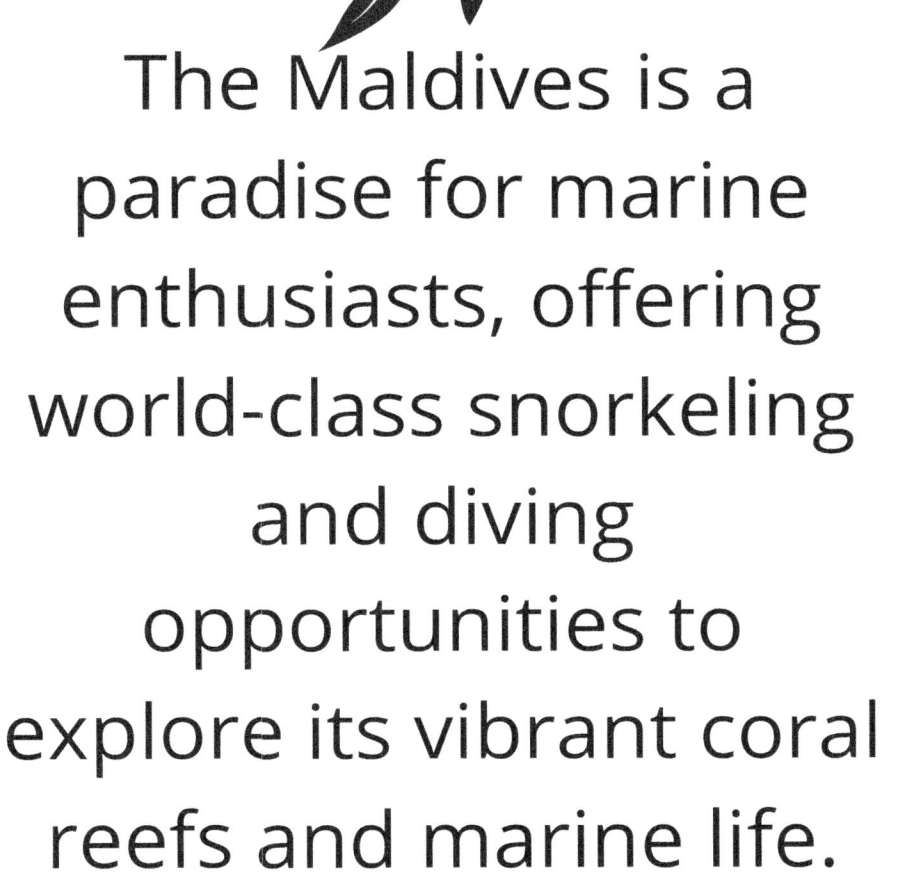

The Maldives is a paradise for marine enthusiasts, offering world-class snorkeling and diving opportunities to explore its vibrant coral reefs and marine life.

The city of Petra, Jordan, once thrived as a bustling trading hub, where merchants from different corners of the world exchanged goods and cultures.

The Arabian Desert's diverse landscape includes not only sand dunes but also vast salt flats, making it a region of surprising geological variety.

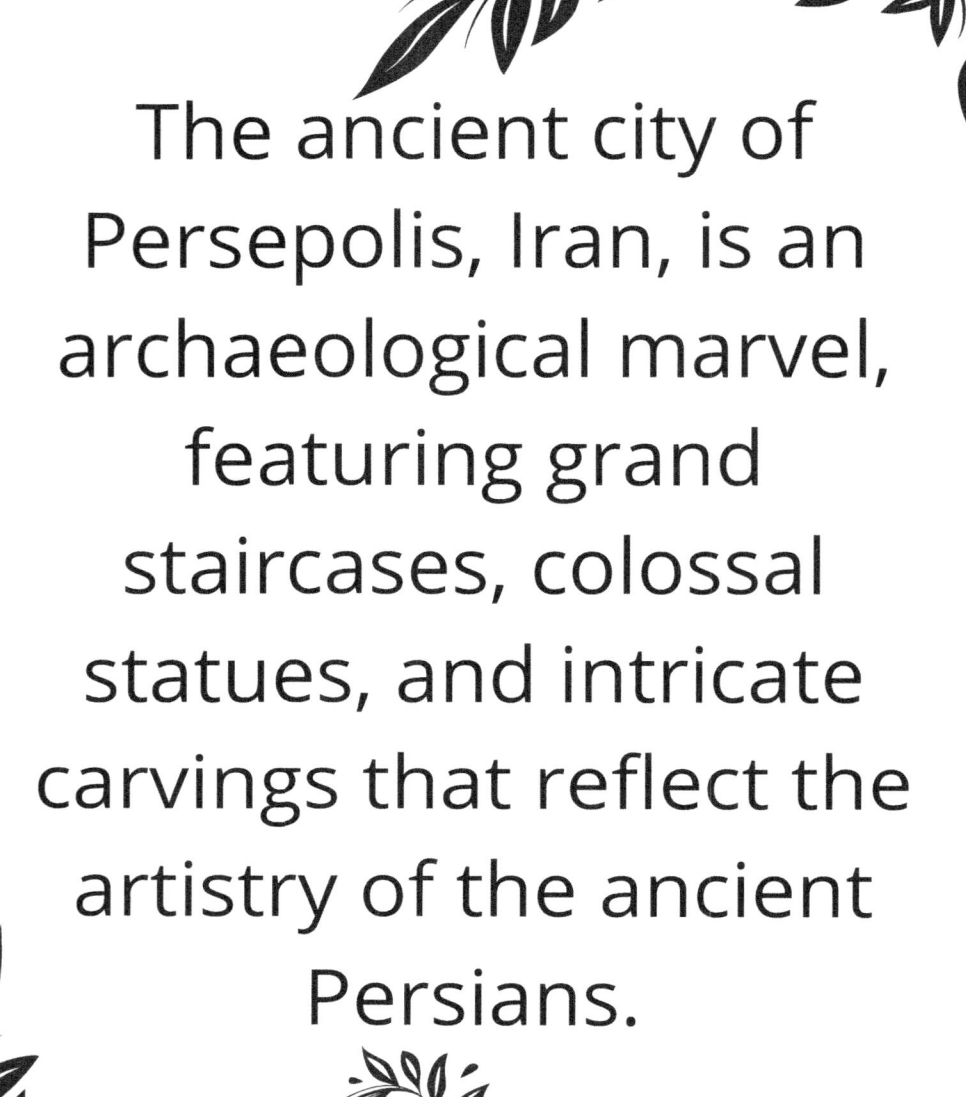

The ancient city of Persepolis, Iran, is an archaeological marvel, featuring grand staircases, colossal statues, and intricate carvings that reflect the artistry of the ancient Persians.

The Maldives' overwater bungalows provide a unique and luxurious experience, with direct access to the crystal-clear waters of the Indian Ocean.

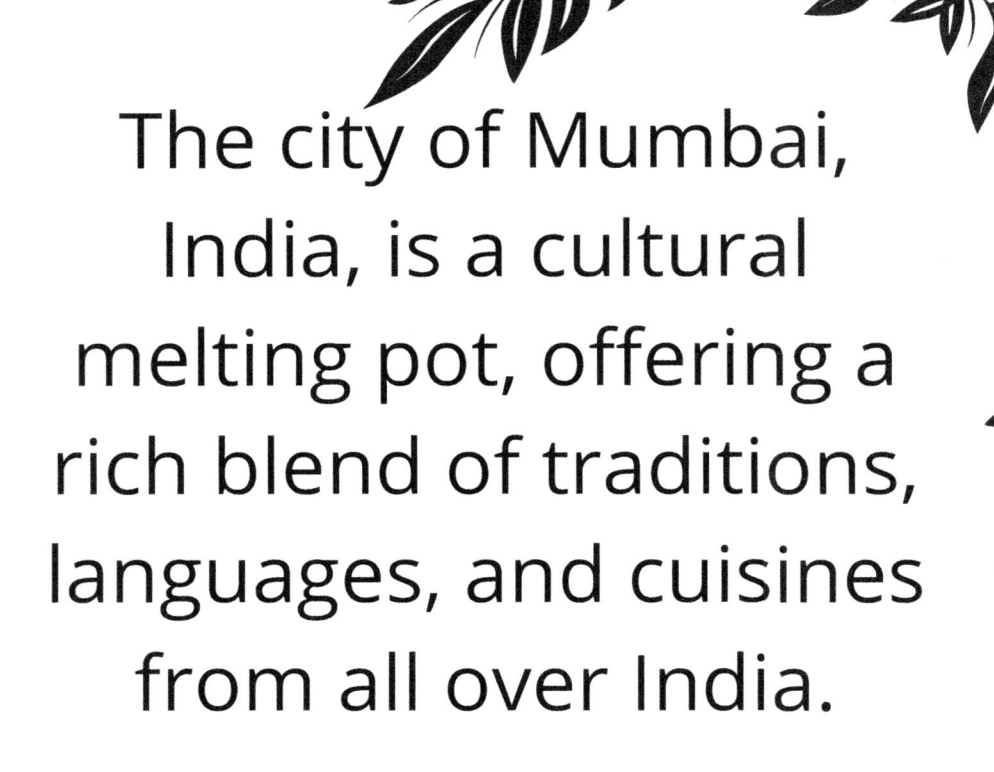

The city of Mumbai, India, is a cultural melting pot, offering a rich blend of traditions, languages, and cuisines from all over India.

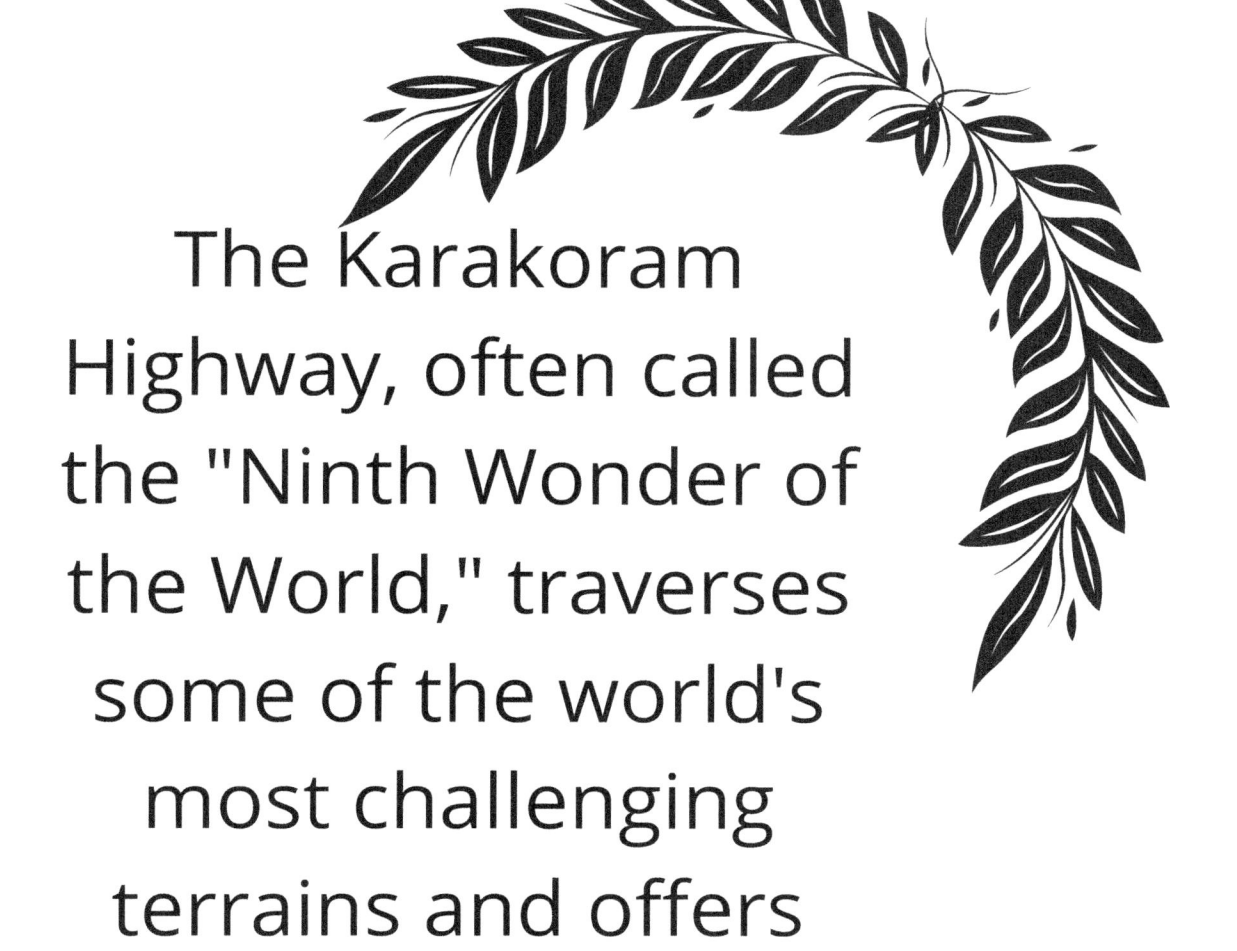

The Karakoram Highway, often called the "Ninth Wonder of the World," traverses some of the world's most challenging terrains and offers breathtaking views of towering peaks.

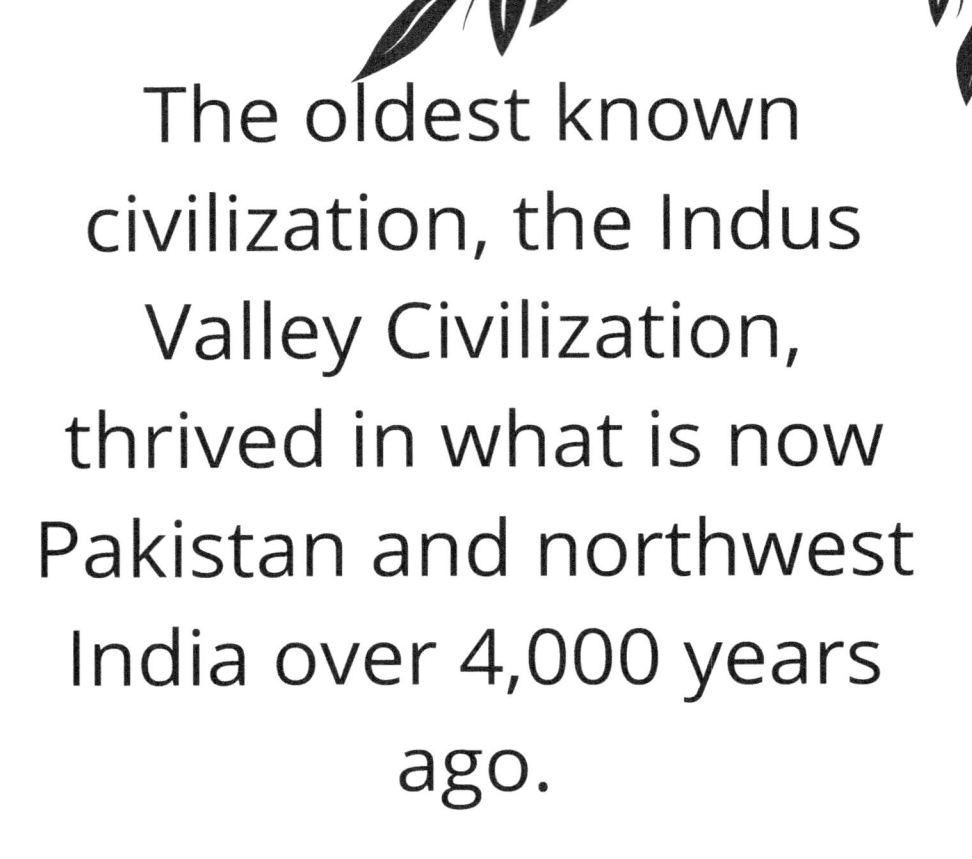

The oldest known civilization, the Indus Valley Civilization, thrived in what is now Pakistan and northwest India over 4,000 years ago.

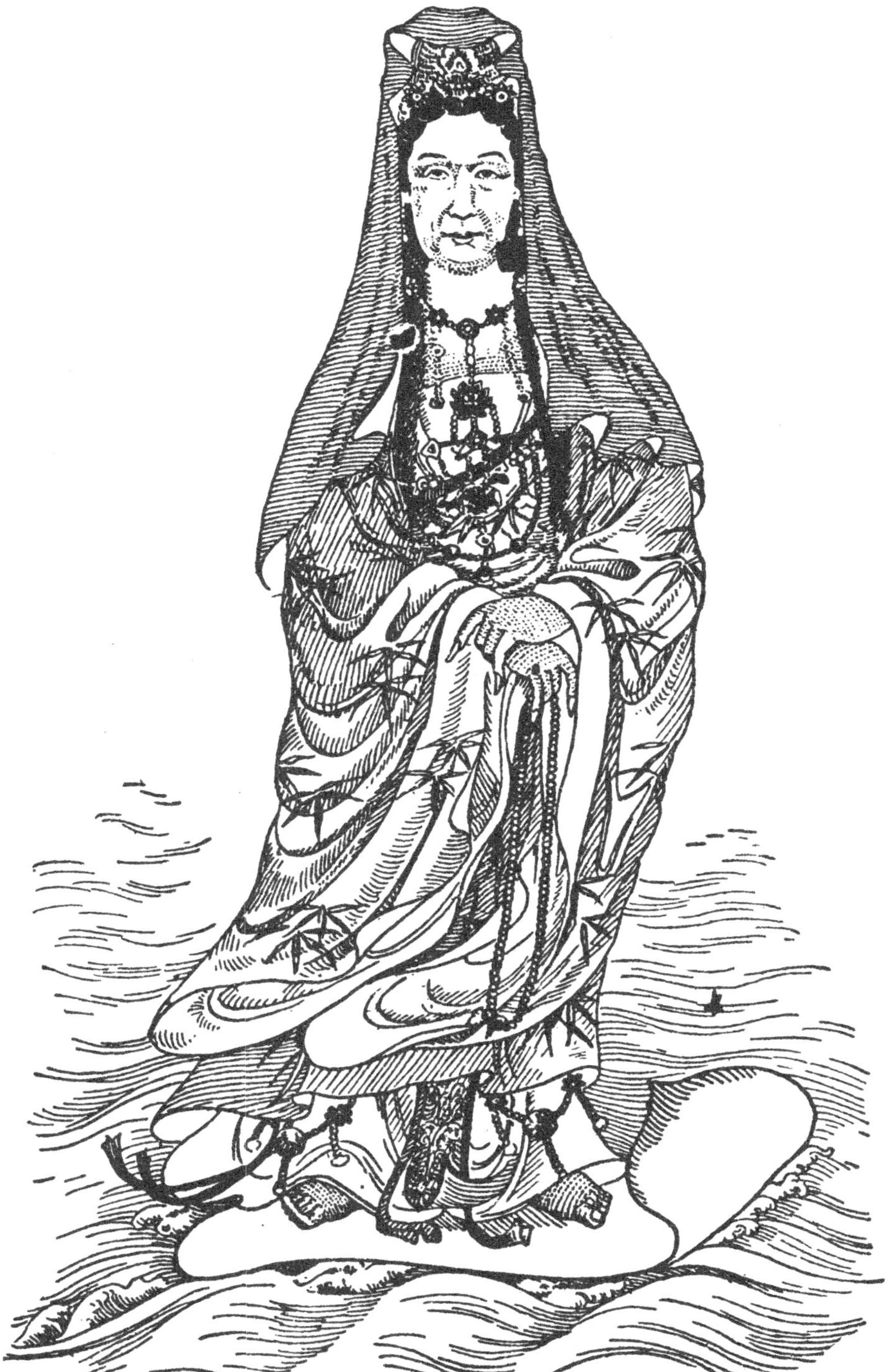

The Silk Road, a vast network of trade routes, connected Asia with Europe, facilitating the exchange of goods, culture, and ideas.

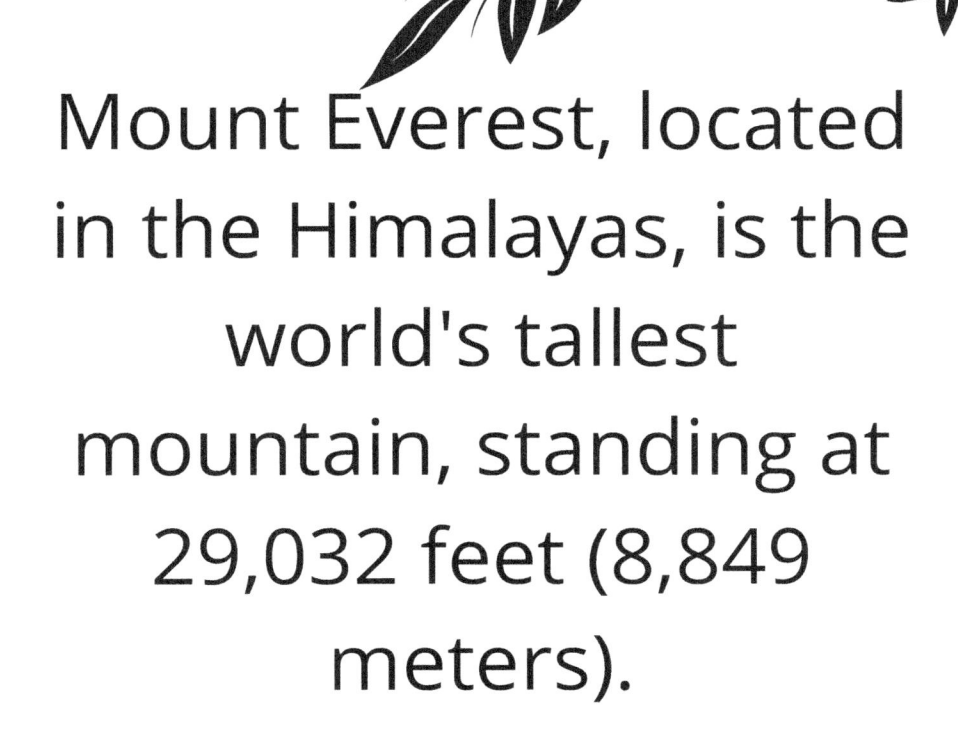

Mount Everest, located in the Himalayas, is the world's tallest mountain, standing at 29,032 feet (8,849 meters).

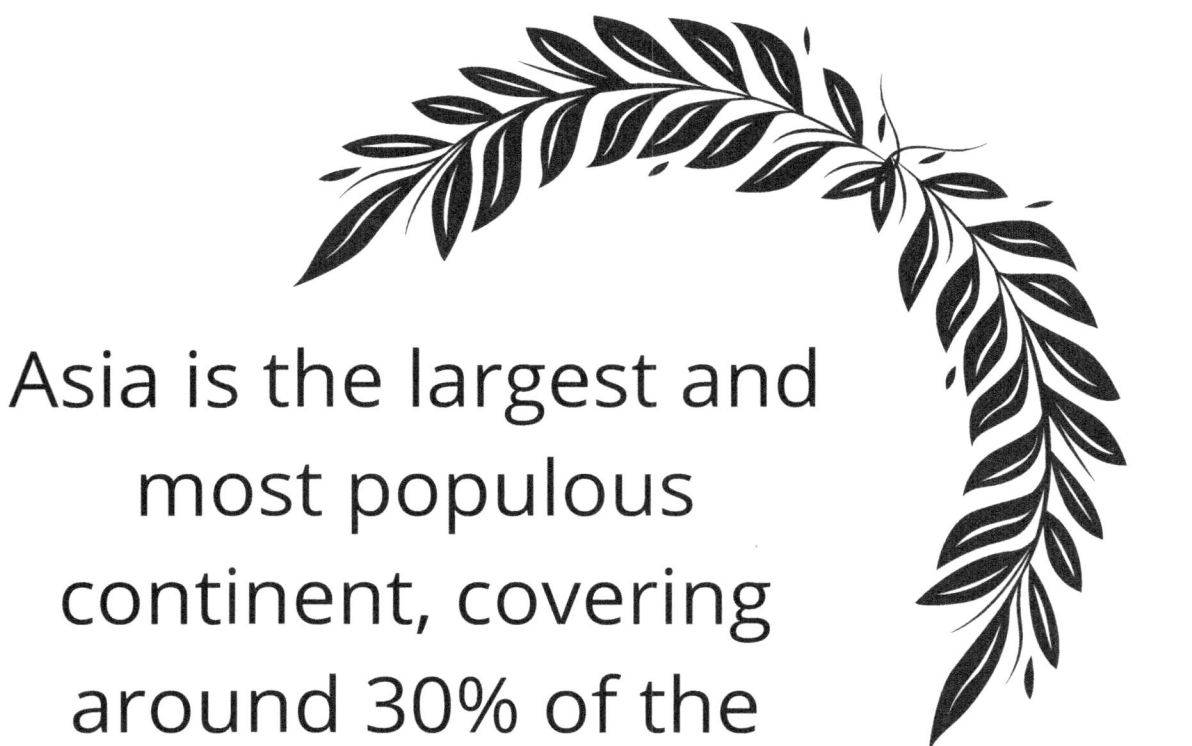

Asia is the largest and most populous continent, covering around 30% of the Earth's land area and hosting over 4.6 billion people.

he highest temperature ever recorded on Earth was 159.3°F (70.7°C) in Furnace Creek Ranch, Death Valley, California, in 1913.

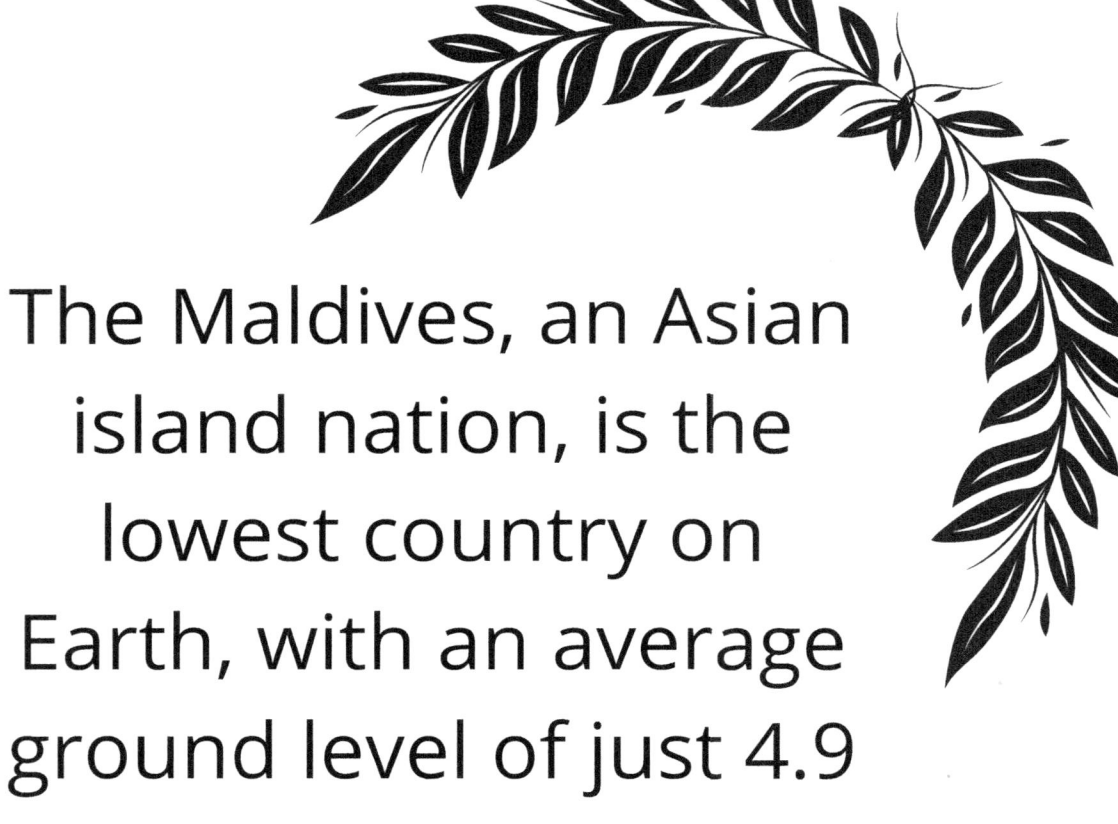

The Maldives, an Asian island nation, is the lowest country on Earth, with an average ground level of just 4.9 feet (1.5 meters) above sea level.

India is the birthplace of major religions like Hinduism, Buddhism, Jainism, and Sikhism.

The Terracotta Army in Xi'an, China, consists of over 8,000 life-sized statues of soldiers, horses, and chariots, created to protect the tomb of Emperor Qin Shi Huang.

The city of Dubai in the United Arab Emirates is known for its incredible architectural wonders, including the Burj Khalifa, the world's tallest building.

Mount Fuji in Japan is an active volcano and a symbol of Japan, often depicted in art and literature.

The ancient city of Petra in Jordan is famous for its rock-cut architecture and was featured in the film "Indiana Jones and the Last Crusade."

Thailand is home to the world's largest solid gold Buddha statue, weighing approximately 5.5 tons.

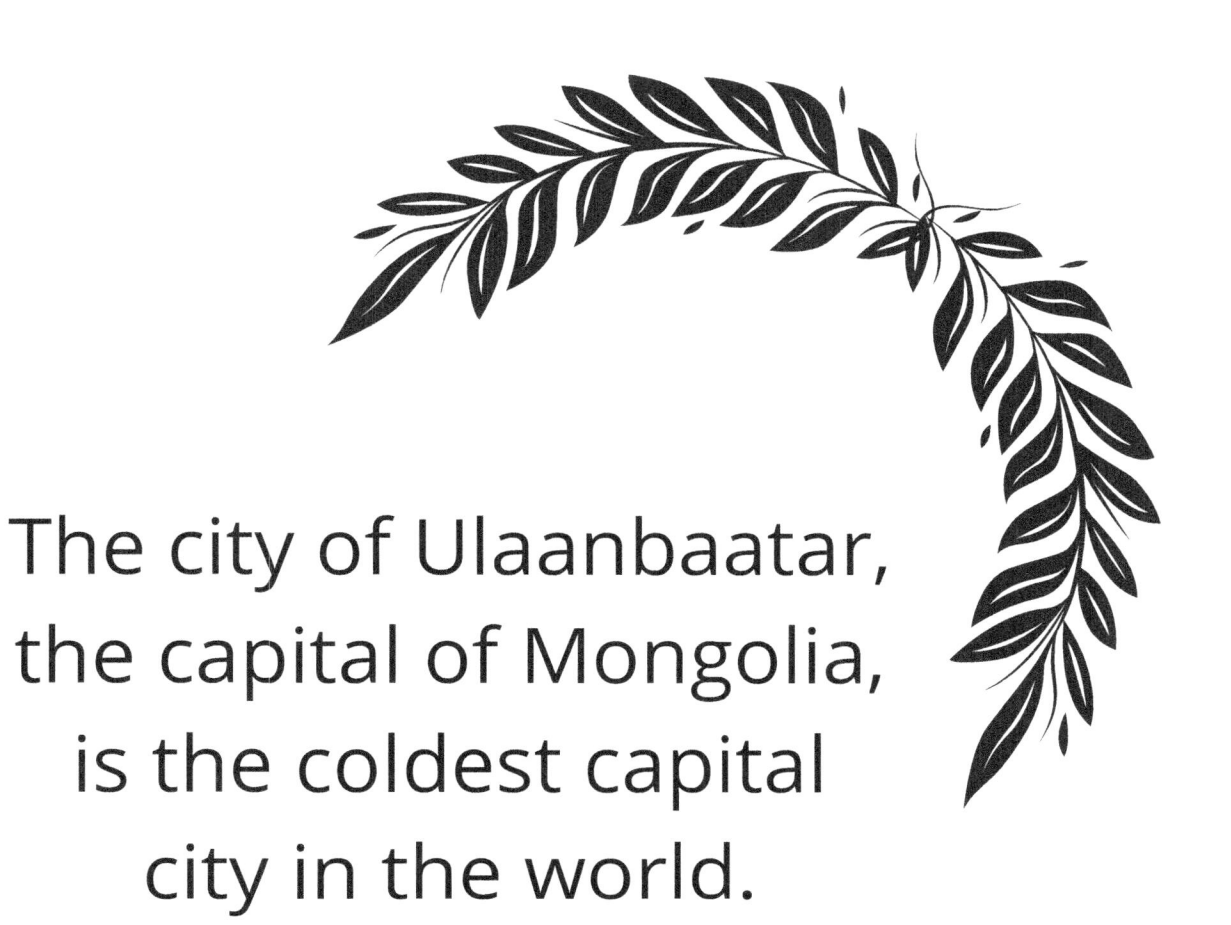

The city of Ulaanbaatar, the capital of Mongolia, is the coldest capital city in the world.

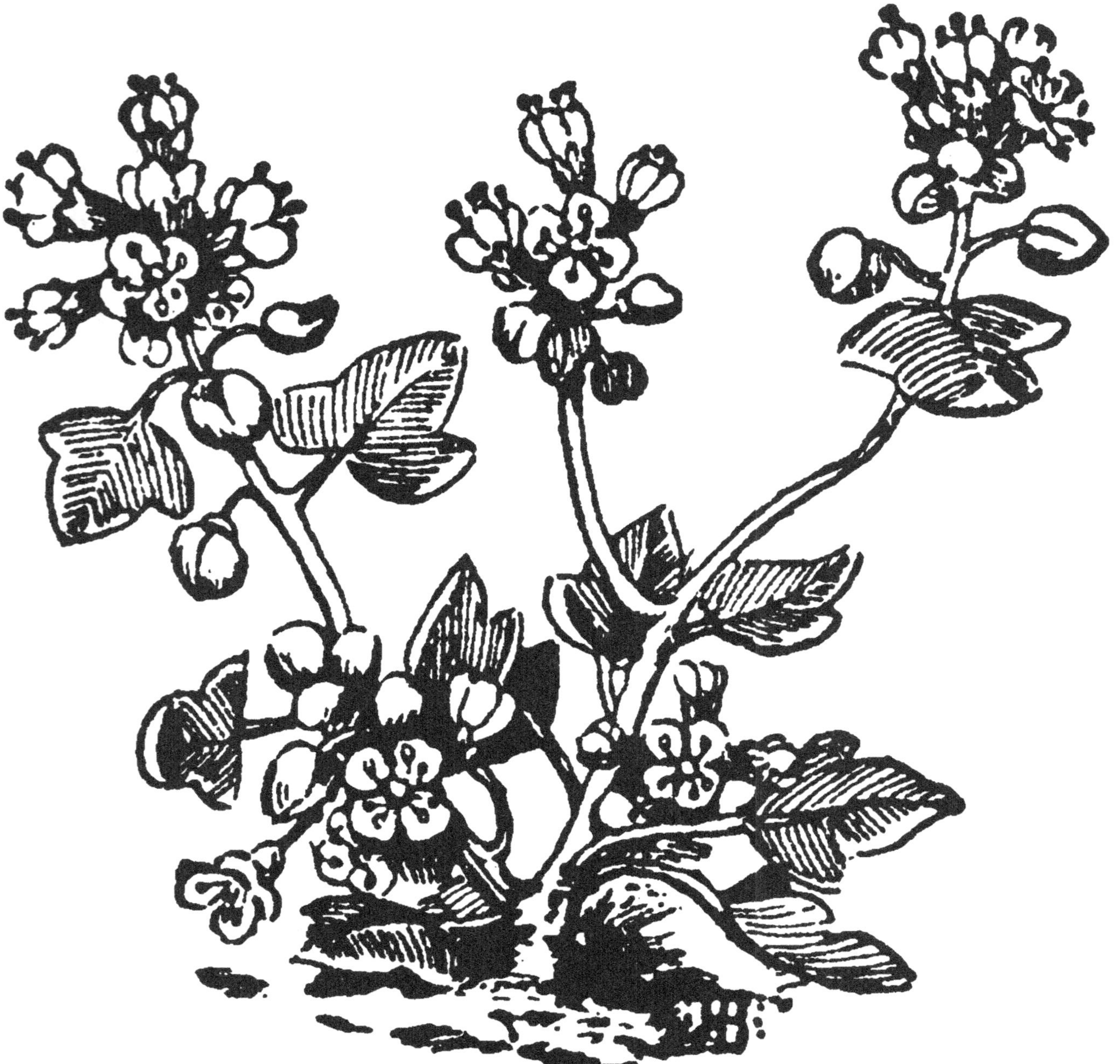

The Komodo dragon, the world's largest living lizard, is native to Indonesia and can grow up to 10 feet in length.

Angkor Wat in Cambodia is the largest religious monument in the world and was originally constructed as a Hindu temple.

The Indonesian island of Java is the most populous island in the world.

The Forbidden City in Beijing, China, is a vast palace complex that served as the imperial palace for Chinese emperors for over 500 years.

The ancient city of Babylon in Iraq was home to the Hanging Gardens, one of the Seven Wonders of the Ancient World.

The city of Lhasa in Tibet is one of the highest-altitude cities globally, sitting at around 12,000 feet (3,656 meters) above sea level.

The ancient city of Persepolis in Iran was the ceremonial capital of the Achaemenid Empire and is a UNESCO World Heritage Site.

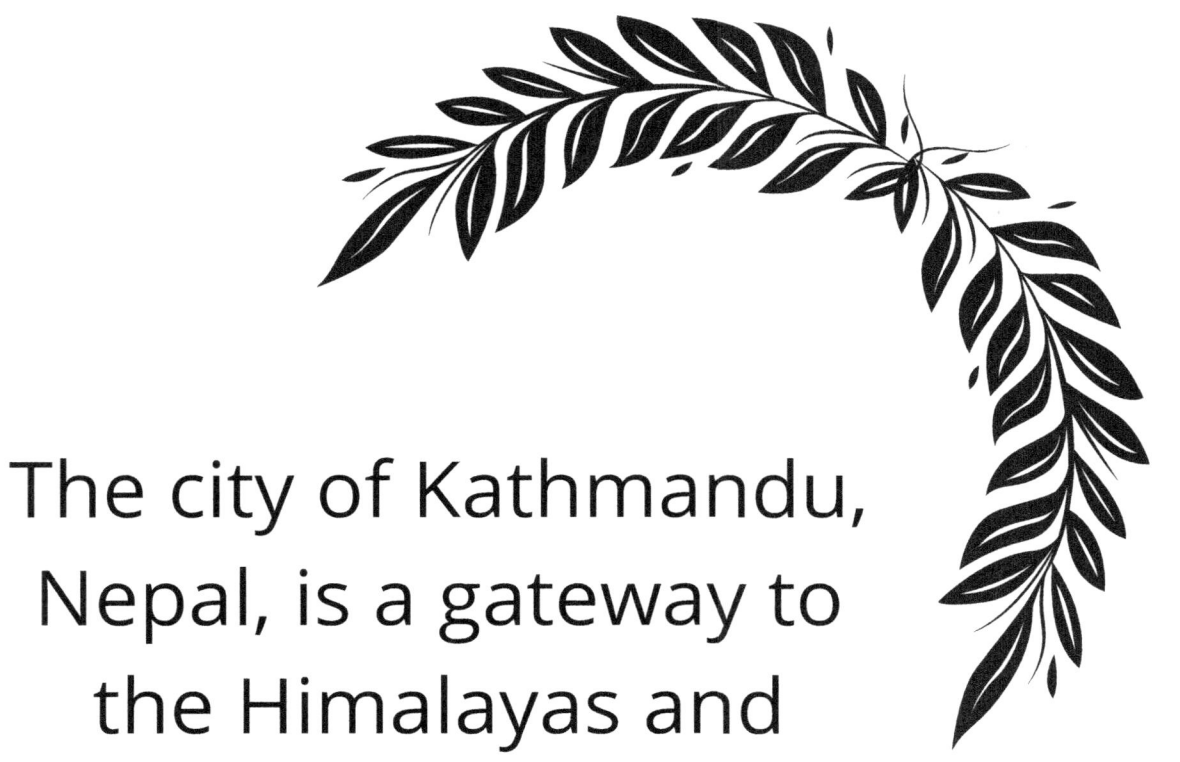

The city of Kathmandu, Nepal, is a gateway to the Himalayas and serves as a hub for trekkers and mountaineers.

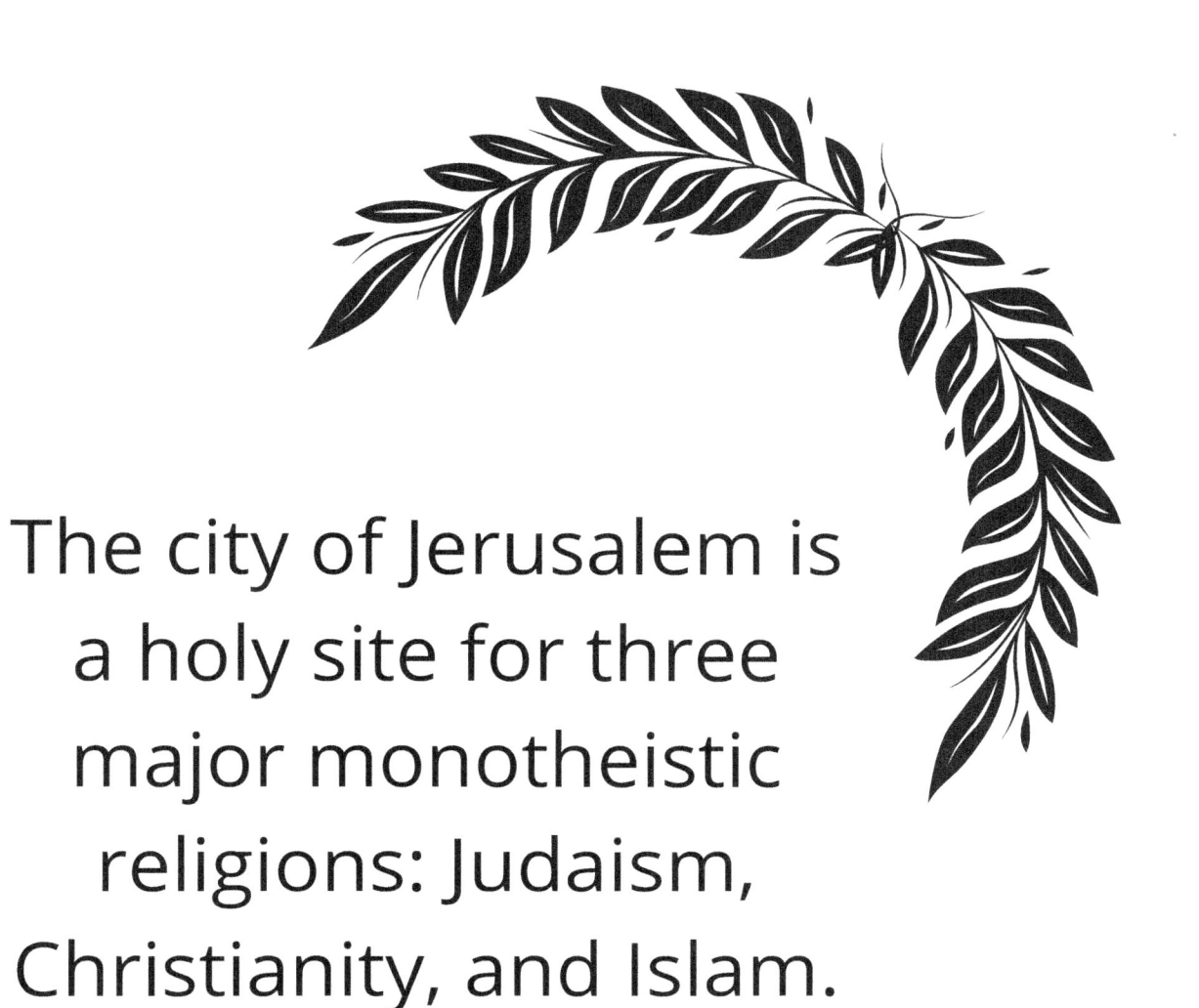

The city of Jerusalem is a holy site for three major monotheistic religions: Judaism, Christianity, and Islam.

Bhutan is the world's first and only carbon-negative country, meaning it absorbs more carbon dioxide than it emits.

The Korean War began in 1950 when North Korean forces invaded South Korea, leading to a conflict that lasted for three years.

The Korean War began in 1950 when North Korean forces invaded South Korea, leading to a conflict that lasted for three years.

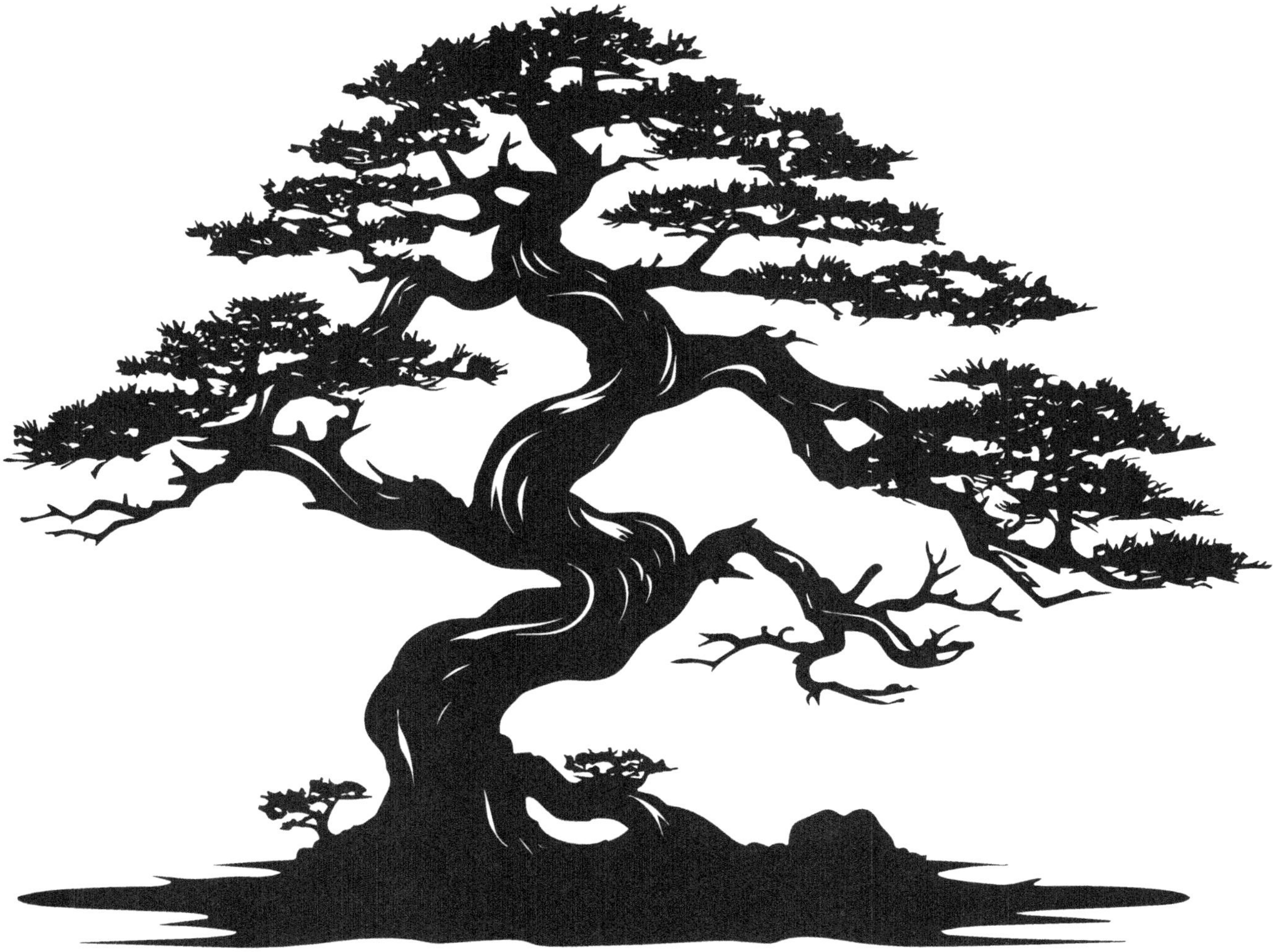

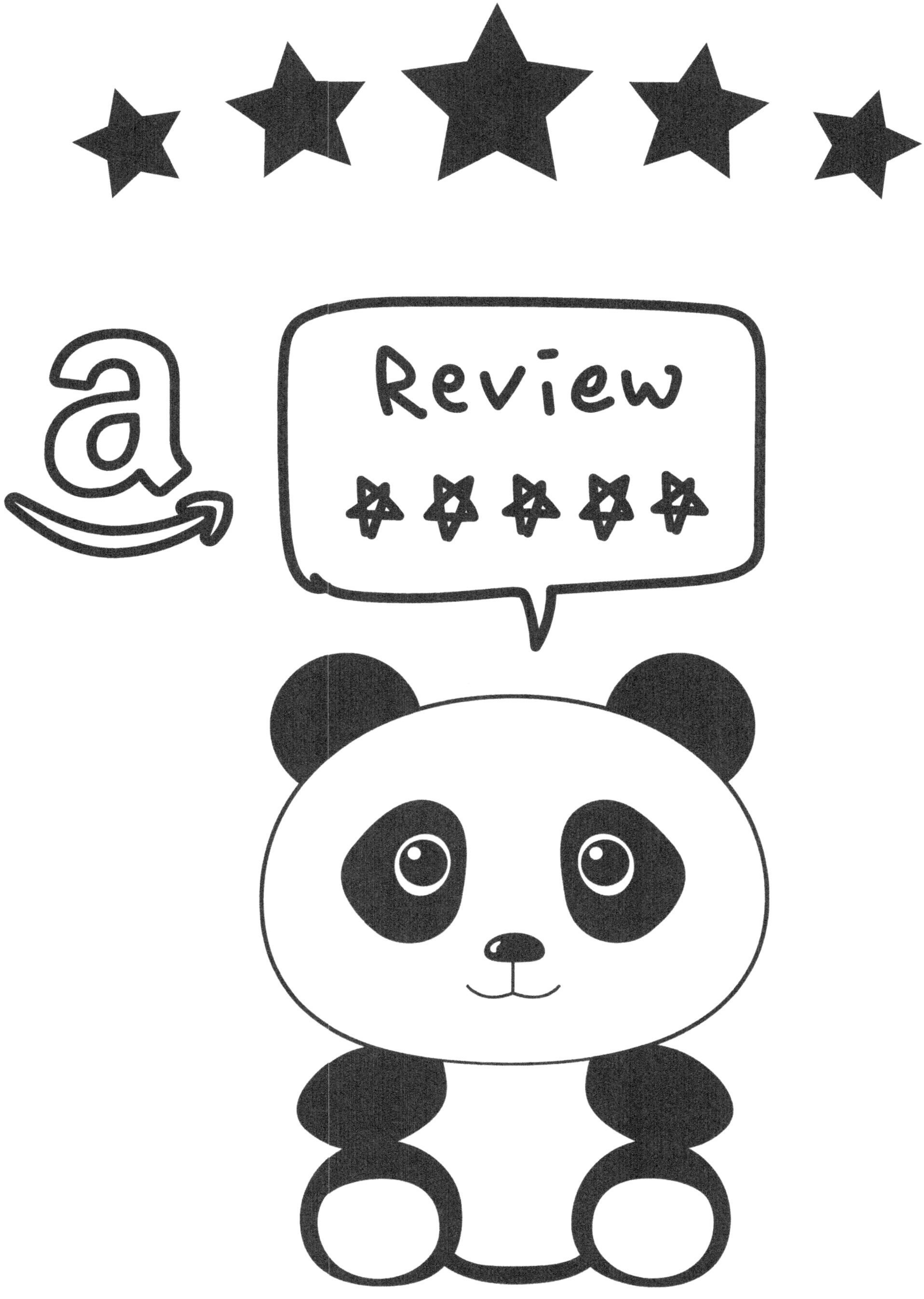
Review

Thank you for joining us on this journey through the diverse and captivating continent of Asia. We hope that the 100 facts presented in this book have illuminated the rich history, cultures, and natural beauty that define this extraordinary land.

As you close this book, we encourage you to explore Asia further, whether through travel, reading, or personal discovery. The wonders of Asia are boundless, and there is always more to learn, experience, and appreciate.

We'd like to express our gratitude to the people and places that make Asia so enchanting, and to our readers for embarking on this adventure with us. It is our hope that this book has deepened your understanding and appreciation of Asia, fostering a sense of wonder and curiosity that will continue to enrich your life.

Stay curious, keep exploring, and may your journey through the diverse and enchanting world of Asia never truly end.

Safe travels,

John Hick

Printed in Great Britain
by Amazon